The Business of Winning

A MANAGER'S GUIDE
TO BUILDING
A CHAMPIONSHIP TEAM
AT WORK

The Business of Winning

A MANAGER'S GUIDE TO BUILDING A CHAMPIONSHIP TEAM AT WORK

Robert Evangelista

CEP Press
A division of
The Center for Effective Performance, Inc.

Atlanta, Georgia

OTHER BOOKS PUBLISHED BY CEP PRESS

Analyzing Performance Problems, Third Edition, by Robert F. Mager &
   Peter Pipe
Conquering Organizational Change: How to Succeed Where Most
   Companies Fail, by Pierre Mourier & Martin Smith
What Every Manager Should Know About Training, by Robert F. Mager

For more information, contact:
CEP Press
A division of The Center for Effective Performance, Inc.
2300 Peachford Rd.
Suite 2000
Atlanta, GA 30338
www.ceppress.com
(770) 458-4080 or (800) 558-4CEP

ISBN 1-879618-21-4

Library of Congress Catalog Card Number: 00-135123

Printed in the United States of America

09 08 07 06 05 04 03 02 01   10 9 8 7 6 5 4 3 2 1

To my coaches in life,
Mom & Dad

And to my life-long teammates,
John, Andrew & Scamp

CONTENTS

Acknowledgments

anaging a sports team and a work team is tough enough. But writing a book was an entirely new challenge to me. The product of 2½ years of work, this book has become the ultimate contrast of experiences: a proud, satisfying achievement and a lengthy and sometimes frustrating effort as well. Anyone who has ever attempted to write a book well knows the work that goes into it. And in keeping with the context of this book, I would like to acknowledge the team that contributed to its creation.

While they will get plenty of mention throughout this book, the entire Detroit Rockies hockey team deserves special mention. Without them, there would be no book. In fact, without the experience and growth from my years with them, I would be far less of a manager, let alone a person. Specifically, Gloria Myers, George Adams, and Alex Gaston were three of the most significant people to enter my life at any time. I am forever indebted to them.

Similar thanks must go to my teams at work. They deserve the praise that should come with their accomplishments. While there are too many names to list, Don Lundberg, Mike Mrozovich, Dan Pacholski, Ed Gaston, Dan Fournier, and Chuck Tyler (posthumously) rate special mention as key players on this team.

There are many people who helped me develop my management style at General Motors, while teaching me their own "tricks of the trade." Larry Spiegel, Jack Armstrong, Denny Bloss, and Brian Leek have all had a significant impact on my growth as a manager. One in particular, Bob Maley, has been my best friend as well as my mentor.

When a brief manuscript of mine began to grow, there was one person who helped me to see that it had the potential to become a book. Kate Newton was more than just my first editor. This book gained character, emotion, and tone from her input. She helped me make the Rockies' story come alive.

A group of managers was generous with their time in performing early reviews of this book. Many of them went out of their way to provide valuable and detailed opinions about the material. Their insights and perspectives became important input that helped make this book a practical guide. Paul Smith, Christopher Sorce, Christopher Robinson, Barbara Rübel, Jeffrey Hagerty, Mike Reidenbach, and Thomas Bennett all formed this panel of reviewers. I am grateful to all of them.

This book benefited from the experienced opinions of members of the book publishing industry. Brooke O'Donnell and Jason Maynard from Independent Publishers Group, along with Bill Hushion and Jules Beauregard from Hushion House (Canada), all contributed their input to final details of this product.

Much of the internal design work, as well as final editing, was performed with exceptional efficiency and flair by Sherry Roberts. She was able to grasp my message and help lay it out so that it became one that flowed easily .

Of course, writing the book was one thing, but getting the world to look at it was quite another. For that task, I was fortunate to have the help of the people at Rocks-Dehart. Celia Rocks quickly gained my trust and was instrumental in helping this book see the light of day.

Throughout the past 2½ years, I've had the support of many friends. They provided encouragement, enthusiasm, and optimism at times when I needed it. Michael Kerske, Ben and Darlene Langlinais, and John Slowik were always a source of energy for me throughout this process. Three other friends contributed additionally. While his cover art suggestions never rated, Gary Truesdale did win the "Name This Book" contest. And Kathy Scheel was not only one of my strongest supporters but one of the book reviewers, as well. Christine Litchard gave me emotional support throughout the early writing and believed in it all along. An aggressive, successful manager with a love for sports, she was always my mental model for this book's target audience. All of these people played an important role in the evolution of this book.

Of course, I must acknowledge the folks at CEP Press, the publishers of this book. A subsidiary of The Center for Effective Performance, Inc., in Atlanta, Georgia, they have made my dreams come true. This professional group of people did more than just develop this project; they put their hearts into it. Ann Parkman, Valerie Gernazian, Paula Alsher, Brady Hill, Paige Gomez, Vicki Chin, Samantha Gitlan, Jill Russell, Leanne McCormick, and all the wonderful people at CEP made this book a true team effort.

I could have wasted a lot of time trying to make my book fit in with some other publisher. Thankfully, I was lucky to be introduced to Dr. Seth Leibler. As the president and CEO of The Center for Effective Performance, he embodies the CEP team's experience, professionalism, and heart. He is a visionary expert in the area of performance improvement and management. His insights into this book have helped to make it a legitimate work. I was sold on CEP minutes after meeting him, and remain so today.

Throughout the last year, there have been many proud moments as this book came together. I would have enjoyed them anyway. However, I have learned how to celebrate life in ways that I never have before. I owe this all to Susan Munaco, who has been nothing short of a godsend to me. She has transformed my life beyond what this book ever could have.

Finally, there is one person to whom I owe my deepest gratitude. Three years ago, this book was just an idea—one that would come out occasionally, but always returned to the dream closet of my mind. I had always been a writer in my heart, but had never actually exercised that notion beyond my experience as the editor of my university's newspaper. For many years since graduation, my urges to write were always suppressed by the needs of my career. And then I talked to Suzanne Bennett. A phone call from out of the blue began a reacquaintance with the one person who worked as hard on our college newspaper as I did. Her inquiries into my writing brought out my fledgling idea for a book. From that moment on, she encouraged me, inspired me, and coached me towards this accomplishment. She has become my biggest supporter, my professional partner, and a dear friend. This book would not exist if it were not for her. She gave me the confidence to attempt it and the perseverance to complete it. Words can never fully express my appreciation to her. (In what is one of the most bizarre and justifiable coincidences, Suzanne is now the publisher of CEP Press.)

We are truly the products of our environments. People enter into our lives and affect us in ways that we may never fully comprehend. For some of us, there will come moments of reflection where we look back at all who have touched our lives and pay special tribute to them. This has been one of those moments for me.

Thank you to all who have contributed to this book. It is as much a part of you as it is of me.

PARTICIPATING IN ATHLETIC COMPETITION *is an analogy for real life. You have to prepare for it. Then you go through the event. Then there's the post-event. It's like life. That's why sports are so special.*

— DR. THOMAS TUTKO
PROFESSOR OF SPORTS PSYCHOLOGY
SAN JOSE STATE UNIVERSITY

Introduction

*L*ike many of you, I walk into my office each morning with the same challenge: to get the best possible results from my organization. As managers in today's intensely competitive and global environment, we don't often have the luxury of time. Results must come quickly, and they must be consistent. Customers have to be satisfied, and owners must make a profit.

As simple as this may sound, we all know achieving those results is fraught with difficulty. Managing and directing people is no easy task. The complexity of the human character ensures that every day we face unique challenges in motivating each employee. We must deal with employees' strengths and weaknesses, their egos and emotions, their good and bad days. Collectively, it is the definition of diversity. And it is our mission to focus, inspire, and direct. On top of all that, and more often than we would like, there are stakeholders, supervisors, and boards of directors who also demand results from us. This makes managing both frustratingly difficult when we fail and richly rewarding when we succeed.

As the manager of a $45 million dollar manufacturing operation for General Motors, I often find myself struggling with these challenges. Many times I have become frustrated while trying to bring some semblance of order to chaos. I've perhaps spent too much time trying to eliminate incompetence where it seemed destined to occur. On too many occasions, I've watched the best laid plans disintegrate as a result of poor preparation and execution. Reflecting on my earlier years, I can't say that I was a great manager back then. However, after the transformation involved with the lessons in this book, I have become a successful manager. When all is said and done, all I really want to be able to say is that with time, experience, and knowledge, I am always improving.

For sixteen years, I had been trying to define my management style and develop my own supervisory techniques. I studied the approaches of various management gurus. I tested their approaches through trial and error. But despite my earnest efforts, I failed to become the manager I hoped to be and started to seriously reassess my approach to management. Having read countless books and tried multitudes of strategies without success, I decided to study the one manager whom I hadn't spent enough time learning from: me.

While searching for clues to help with my professional life, I spent some time examining my personal life. Introspection led me to compare my work activities as a manager to one aspect of my personal life: coaching. A few years earlier, I had assumed the head coaching duties for a traveling hockey team of inner-city teenagers playing in the Southeast Michigan area. After endless hours of practicing and learning new skills, the team suddenly began to experience tremendous success in the arena. This new triumph was an exciting and invigorating experience for me, yet it contrasted so sharply with my professional performance that I couldn't help but wonder how I could be so happy and successful at the hockey rink, and yet so frustrated and ineffectual at the office.

As I examined my two worlds, the truth quickly became apparent. I was far more successful at coaching than I was at managing. In fact, I actually liked myself much better as a coach. As I pondered this new insight, I realized just how different my coaching and managing styles really were. I was especially disappointed in myself when I realized that coaching a sports team and managing an organization were so much alike. Intrigued, I began to make notes of my observations about managing people in the workplace, and soon the sports parallel took shape. It became obvious that I was applying completely different management approaches in two nearly identical situations!

In an effort to remedy the situation, I began applying management techniques drawn from my coaching repertoire to my professional life. Daily I searched for new opportunities to apply my coaching methods in the workplace and, upon discovering them, took specific actions in the office that mirrored my approach in the hockey rink. The number of opportunities was staggering. Nothing, however, was as phenomenal and unexpected as the success that followed. In a mere fourteen months, my faltering "team" at GM achieved extraordinary success, with impressive gains in productivity, cost savings, quality, and safety. We far surpassed previous accomplishments. Our productivity rose 52 percent, our first-time quality rose more than 40 percent, our scrap and repair costs were cut in half, and we reduced our operating expenses by 25 percent, all while reducing our manpower needs by 33 percent. There's nothing to be bashful about—we had a hell of a year!

Considering how many people are involved in or watch sports, it's amazing that the parallel between sports and management isn't explored and applied more often in the business arena. The concepts and techniques behind good coaching can be easily applied to managing. If you have ever watched, read about, or played sports, you will recognize many of the concepts that are in this book. It might not have been obvious to you before as to how these techniques can apply to management. If you've never been a sports fan, then you're on the verge of a new understanding of team management. By discovering the parallels between coaching players and managing employees, you too may understand how to apply simple concepts that make sense to work situations that don't.

It is refreshing for many of us to find that learning from sports coaching can improve our performance at work. Seldom do our personal worlds ever get to complement our professional ones. As for me, I always thought I'd find the ultimate management solutions in a colorfully bound volume from my local bookstore. Little did I know that those lessons would instead find me at a ramshackle hockey rink in west Detroit.

What Will It Take to Win at Work?

OUR BEST EFFORTS, *combined with those of our teammates, grow into something far greater and far more satisfying than anything we could have achieved on our own. Teams make us a part of something that matters. They are the fountain from which all our rewards will ultimately flow.*

— PAT RILEY, NBA COACH, MIAMI HEAT

For some of us, management gets pretty frustrating at times. Take a look for a moment at the management approach of your own organization. You may believe what I did at first: that we as managers are doing the right things. We put a lot of effort into defining our goals for the entire organization. Our mission statements are crafted, and our goals are identified and quantified. Then, we communicate to everyone what those objectives are and that they must help to meet them. New projects come along, new accounts are created, and targets are quantified. We make sure that everyone understands their expectations. We send them to training to give them the skills. And then we concentrate on monitoring people's performance, sales levels, project funding, deadlines, etc. After the customer is served, we share feedback with our employees regarding customer satisfaction, company results, or their own performance. And we strive to continuously improve every aspect of our task.

And yet some of us still are unsuccessful. Why?

Simply put, we have forgotten that business is a team game, not an individual one. While there may be many individual tasks or functions within the business, such as those associated with sales, consulting, or programming, the sum of the parts is not always greater than the whole. Somewhere along the way, all of the individuals must come together to become one complete organization, unified in their focus, their preparation, and their execution. The organization as a whole has to actually accomplish something. Too much emphasis on managing the performance of individuals can cloud a manager's vision. While improving individual performance is critical to building a winning team, that strategy will not result in success on its own.

Think about it in the context of team sports. If a football coach only concentrated on the individual players, then what would result? Might the physical capability of the individual players improve? Perhaps. Would the team's ability to execute their plays as one unified group be any better? I doubt it. Additionally, think about the coach's job. Think about how much more difficult it is to have to teach every individual, one at a time. Put yourself in the coach's shoes. Would you be able to spend enough time with each member of your team so that each player not only fully comprehends the team philosophy, the overall strategies of the game plan, and the purpose of their individual roles in the playing unit, but can also excel at it? Better call home because you'll be working late!

It becomes obvious that a manager of a group of people, regardless of size, must comprehend how to lead the complete group. Total success will only come if everyone is contributing. Therefore, the manager's challenge is similar to that of the coach: how to motivate people to do their part to the best of their ability in a way that contributes to the team's ultimate goal.

When many of us are first promoted into management roles, we receive little preparation on how to develop, motivate, and improve individual performance. We get even fewer clues on how to do that for the whole group. MBA programs may teach us to deal with quantitative aspects of business, but they don't teach us how to focus, develop, motivate, and drive a team of employees. Look around and you'll see the same trends. New managers are promoted all the time by higher managers who have the best intentions to train, develop, and nurture their leadership neophytes. However, the needs of the business often subordinate these intentions, and pretty soon, we're all holding the fire hose trying to put out fires. So businesses end up introducing new managers into their positions without really preparing them to manage.

Similar to the novice, many of us who have been at this game for years still struggle because of inadequate people management skills. Our methods are derived from imitating the actions of managers who we've worked for, along with plenty of trial and error. The tactics we need aren't taught in too many places. Sure, we get better at it as we go along; however, the needs of our customers and shareholders usually determine our personal improvement rates to be inadequately slow.

There are, of course, other avenues for managers to get advice. Many management books deal with the difficult task of managing employees. Unfortunately, few of them give any insight into how managing individual performance fits into managing the overall performance of the organization. In fact, as a coach, I am insulted by the number of management books that talk about "coaching" but only with respect to individual performance. There is this mistaken belief that "coaching," as it pertains to management, only applies to the teaching and development of one employee at a time.

But, you might wonder, what if I have a group of people who aren't working together as a team, but are all doing their jobs as defined? An organization comprised of individuals, acting, thinking and executing only what *they* believe they need to do cannot succeed easily. People *only* doing their job is not enough. In fact, the only way for an organization of narrowly focused, individualistic employees to easily succeed as a group is for them to be led by one incredibly omnipotent, omnipresent, and omniscient manager. It will be up to this "super" manager to coordinate all of their efforts and focus every activity. Additionally, it will be up to the manager to steer the organization, since he or she will be the only one who truly knows where and how it must go forward. I'm sure that many of you, like me, don't want to work *that* hard.

Consider this: What kind of organization do you ultimately want to create? Do you want an organization filled with individuals who can achieve predefined targets and then step back and wait for new marching orders? Or do you want an organization that operates independent of constant direction, focuses on goals, and executes its defined roles in a team environment according to an overall plan?

That's the difference! And that's our greatest challenge. Creating a team that can run by itself. Developing inside every individual the comprehension of an overall plan. Generating the intensity inside each individual to accomplish his or her own tasks *in support* of a larger effort. Having employees so focused and understanding of their roles that they seem to operate as if they're on autopilot. That's what every manager dreams of. That's the Management Holy Grail. And to get it, you must build a winning team!

This is where many of us managers "hit the wall." Once employees are performing their tasks and accomplishing an overall purpose, how do you get to this higher level of performance? While this seems like an imposing question with no simple answer, I have to admit that I learned the answer to that challenge pretty quickly. In fact, it was taught to me by a bunch of teenaged boys.

The Detroit Rockies: The Coaching Experience

I remember the day that a coworker first approached me to talk about hockey. Being a Canadian recently relocated to Michigan, word had spread through the factory that if you wanted to talk hockey, this new manager was the guy. My coworker, Alex Gaston, was coaching a team that consisted of the best teenaged players drawn from the house leagues that played in the Detroit Hockey Association, and he was looking for advice on coaching the team. His son played on the team, and he had coached this same group of kids as they progressed over the years. Prior to that point, Alex had known nothing about hockey. As he had explained it, he and two other fathers were "coaches by default." His concern was that his boys needed some advanced coaching if they were going to compete at a higher level. He invited me to attend one of their games and check out the Rockies.

I can still remember how amazed I was sitting in the stands watching the team for the first time. The boys had terrific speed and agility. They loved to play physical, and they all shared the same fire. What was particularly odd for me was that every member of the Detroit Rockies was black.

Coming from Canada, I had not been exposed to many black hockey players, so I was particularly astonished. My reaction had nothing to do with stereotypes or prejudices; it was simply a function of the relatively small number of blacks playing this sport throughout the world. Most hockey fans would have the same response. That night, while witnessing (and listening to) some of the additional "challenges" that the kids faced from less open-minded opponents, officials, and opposing fans, I was energized. After watching the Rockies lose to a team that was *only* more organized than they were, I decided to help Alex out.

This team was playing in the highly competitive Little Caesar's Travel Hockey League in Southeast Michigan. The league consisted of teams that were made up of the best hockey players in their cities or hockey associations. If history is an indicator, some of these players would be future professional stars. I was thrilled to get the chance to coach at that high level of youth hockey. At this age group, this was as good as it got.

The Detroit Rockies had some challenges however. The Rockies were the only team to skate within the city limits of Detroit. The arena was small, old, and dilapidated. The boards were crooked and had holes in them. Chain fence rose above the boards where normal arenas had glass. The locker rooms were small and cramped, making it difficult for all fourteen boys to sit down at the same time while getting dressed.

These challenges become significant when you consider that the Southeast Michigan area is comprised of many large cities and suburbs that enjoy family incomes that, on average, are much higher than the nation's average. The hockey associations based in these suburbs were mostly located in newer, updated arenas and had the luxury of having a large talent pool of hockey players from which to choose their best. That was not the case for us. While the Rockies had official tryouts at the beginning of each season, we never actually had enough kids show up to ever have to cut players. So I began my three-year coaching tenure with a group of kids who had plenty of experience on the ice, but had never really learned how to play a team game.

The Rockies' Players

Anyone who has tried to coach a group of teenaged boys in this day and age knows that it's a challenge. In the case of the Rockies, the boys were cocky and full of energy. They talked back, rebelled, and resisted control. They each wanted to be stars. They all wanted to score. And, of course, they wanted to do it their way. They hated practice. They abhorred drills, favoring instead the full-contact scrimmage games at the end of practice sessions.

Away from the arena, they lived in a world that some of us could not relate to. Single mothers, grandparents, or aunts raised many of them. They resisted joining gangs. They said "no" to drugs every day. They had known people who were killed or jailed. They all wanted a future, but could not always see it. Fortunately for them, they had parents, relatives, or guardians that were committed to them. They had someone behind them, scraping together money for team fees and equipment costs, wanting to keep them playing hockey.

They had some other things in common, too. They loved to play hockey. They wanted desperately to win. They all had dreams of being on top some-day. They loved the camaraderie and fed off of it. And they all had big hearts. In the end, that was all that I required as a coach.

Three Years to the Top

I had committed myself to remain with the team until the boys were too old to play. That meant that I would have them from ages fourteen to seven-teen. Not exactly the easiest years to handle.

Alex, the original coach, and George Adams, who also had a son playing on the team, were our assistant coaches. The team manager, Gloria Myers, the mother of one of the players, rounded out our leadership team. She handled all the financial and administrative duties and supported us. We all seemed to talk the same language and took the same approach to our tasks. We all shared the belief that winning or losing was not the ultimate goal. Rather the goal was to help these boys mature into solid, young men with values. (Of course, we wanted to win, too!)

We started off aggressively pursuing those goals. We began applying an approach that is common in team sports coaching: create a solid foundation of fundamental skills and comprehension, and then build complexity upon that base. Our game plan would be basic, but it could always have many options diverging from it. We never wanted to stray from our basic ap-proach. Our players needed to have one style of play completely ingrained in their minds—our style. Their team play needed to be so familiar to them that, in the most frenzied times on the ice, they would reflexively return to where they were supposed to be.

Over the years, they settled into it all. The team practiced the same drills, formations, and plays over and over again. In games, we approached different opponents consistently, with a few "personalized" adjustments. The guys eventually began to play together as a team, with their instincts and knowledge synchronized. We started winning games—finally. And the losses, while becoming fewer in number, contributed to our growth purposefully.

Hockey became a fun game for us to play. I left the arena many nights feeling fulfilled and satisfied to be a part of such terrific improvement.

In the final year, knowing that it was our last year together, we had planned on attending a major hockey tournament in Lake Placid, New York. It was one of the biggest, most popular tournaments in the United States. We were playing good hockey for most of the year, but we were plagued with injuries for much of it. We lost in our attempts to vie for the state championships at a time when four of our best players were sidelined with injuries. However, we were completely healthy for the Lake Placid tournament, which was held a month after our season ended.

At that tournament, something magical happened for all of us. Everything that we had worked for seemed to come together at once. A healthy team of fast, aggressive Rockies put on a show. We overpowered opponents with a combination of speed, aggressiveness, and an opportunistic transitional game. Within two days, our games were attracting locals from the town who were coming to see the "black team from Detroit." By the end of the tournament, we had gone 6-0 and outscored our opponents 35-6 to win the gold medal. To do this in the same arena that witnessed the 1980 Olympic "Miracle on Ice" made it even more special. The boys played their best hockey ever. We defeated teams from New York, California, Minnesota, Michigan, Massachusetts, and Canada.

We raised some eyebrows in Lake Placid. Of course, the fact that ours was a team of young black kids from Detroit only added to the attention we received. Following that tournament, our team and our association were featured in both local and national press. We were mentioned on national TV and cable shows. We even had a movie screenplay written about us that is still circulating in Hollywood.

The Managing Experience

From the emotional highs that defined our Lake Placid experience, I dropped and landed in my troubled office at work. I was a manager struggling to get results out of people who I couldn't seem to focus or motivate. I labored for some time while I adopted management styles that I had learned from my "teachers" throughout the years. Without intending to test their effectiveness, I quickly learned that the modern-day employee does not respond well to some of the old tactics. It became apparent to me that as people change, so must management styles and techniques.

The worker of the seventies and eighties is different from that of today. I began to notice that many older managers were having difficulty inspiring and motivating younger workers. Employees of this modern day are certainly bolder and more inquisitive. They require much more information. It is not enough to be told what to do; they also require the understanding of why they have to do it. And if they don't believe it should be done a certain way, or at all, then they will challenge it. Workers of this era also are looking for a greater sense of self-worth and contribution. They want to feel important. And if the job that they're doing doesn't make them feel important, then they want another one.

Does this attitude make them difficult employees? Or disrespectful? Not necessarily. They're simply members of a dynamic species. They're today's real people. And they're our employees.

While I was coaching, I couldn't help but notice that my kids on the team were similar to many employees at work. They asked "why?" They challenged direction if they didn't understand it. They questioned assignments that they didn't think were glamorous, whining, "Why do I have to be the one to play defense, Coach?" Both at work and at the arena, I found myself having to explain to everyone "why."

Sports players have changed, just like modern employees. In fact, I was impressed by a remark made by Mike Keenan, a coach for many years in the National Hockey League. Talking about the old days of hockey, he said, "In those days, they coached through fear sometimes. You played out of fear for your job. Those days are gone. You could see it changing, even in the late sixties and seventies: more and more, coaches had to have an answer for your questions. It wasn't, 'Do this because I'm your boss,' or 'You're doing this because I told you to do it.' The big difference today is that when a coach asks a player to do something, he has to have an answer, because if he doesn't, why should [the player] have to do it that way?"

For me personally, there was one striking observation that I made when I compared my work team to my team at the arena: I was actually "getting through" to my hockey team. That led to my question, "What was I doing at the arena that helped me motivate my players that I wasn't doing at work with my employees?"

Trying to Coach at Work

"How could I become a coach at work?" I wondered. While at the arena, I began to pay more attention to *how* I was doing what I was doing. I listened to myself talk. I paid attention to how I treated the team. I noticed the emphasis I placed on players' roles and their context in the team. I realized that everything I did with the team was always founded on our overall plan. I surprised myself with all the differences between "Coach Rob" and "Mr. Evangelista."

Conversely, at work, I noticed how there was a definite lack of focus for my team members, as well as for me as their leader. I was not giving them the game plan to achieve success. Nor was I coaching them on how to execute that game plan. My behavior did not seem to be based on any overall plan at all and, therefore, at times was non-contributory. I couldn't point to many instances where I was teaching them their roles and how to play them as a team. In fact, I did little to encourage team play. Instead, I relied on a few major contributors to carry the load, and chastised the ones who weren't contributing.

And because I had done their jobs earlier in my career, I spent too much time giving directions that contained no support. I contributed often to task interference. I micromanaged situations that didn't need me. It was a typical collection of mistakes that come too easily to many managers. At least they came easily to me.

When it all came down to my own personal day of reckoning, I realized that I was trying to turn my employees into *me*. I was trying to create autonomy and independent thinking, when in fact I was eliminating it. I wasn't respecting their own identities, their own specialties, their own uniqueness. I didn't recognize the roles they could have played. I wanted every individual to work the same way, with the same intensity, attention to detail, and proactive thinking.

More importantly though, I realized that I wasn't teaching my people. I wasn't coaching my team! Instead, I *told* them to go out and win the game. I *told* them that they had to score touchdowns and sink baskets in order to win. I told them to keep their eye on the ball and to avoid making errors and taking costly penalties. I told them to bear down and concentrate. I told them it was life or death, that the championship was all that mattered. I pleaded with them to care. And to work harder. And when they lost, I told them they hadn't worked hard enough. Then I would wonder why they never won.

I think back now and I remember the old saying:

"Give a man a fish, he will eat for a day.
Teach a man to fish, he will eat for a lifetime."

Standing in front of my hockey team, I was teaching my boys to "fish." At work, I was telling them they had to go out and fish in order to survive and then giving them hell when they starved to death.

As you can imagine, my self-analysis startled me as I documented all the differences between my two styles. Ultimately, considering the results I was enjoying at the arena, I was faced with altering my management style.

As I began to look around at other managers, I saw many of the same shortcomings. Looking to confirm that my observations existed beyond my own world, I extended my search to include acquaintances from other industries, as well as books on management. I engaged in conversation after conversation with peers who noticed the same deficiencies in their behavior as I had, while also agreeing that the "lessons" I had learned from coaching were indeed relevant.

What Can We Learn from Sports Coaches?

I set out to change my style of management to match my coaching manner more closely. I documented lessons learned behind the bench. I compared differences in techniques and planning methods. I started making notes on what I perceived to be good coaching in the professional leagues. Being an avid sports fan, I knew well the legacies of the great coaches.

Looking to validate my lessons from the arena, I studied professional and collegiate coaches who had been successful, reading many documentaries of their methods. I paid particular attention to the coaches who were able to achieve success consistently while facing much adversity. They are great names associated with great legends:

> ➤ **Vince Lombardi**—NFL coach of the Green Bay
> Packers and the Washington Redskins. He took
> over a Packers team that had gone 1-10-1 in the
> previous season, and within two years, had them
> playing for the championship. Over seven years,
> he won five championships, including three con-
> secutive championships.

➤ **Scotty Bowman**—NHL coach of the St. Louis Blues, Montreal Canadiens, Buffalo Sabres, Pittsburgh Penguins and, currently, the Detroit Red Wings. He has won a record-tying eight Stanley Cup championships as a coach. What makes this unique is that Bowman has accomplished this feat with three different teams.

➤ **John Wooden**—UCLA men's basketball coach during the '60s and '70s. His Bruins won ten NCAA national championships, including seven in a row. Over his career, he amassed a winning percentage of more than 80 percent.

➤ **Anson Dorrance**—University of North Carolina women's soccer coach. In the eighteen years that the NCAA has held a national soccer championship for women, Dorrance's Tar Heels have won fifteen of them.

➤ **Dean Smith**—former head coach of the University of North Carolina men's basketball team for thirty-six years. He holds the college record with 879 wins as a coach, all during a period when he established high moral ethics in a program that saw 97 percent of its players graduate.

➤ **Lou Holtz**—head coach of NCAA men's football teams at Notre Dame and the universities of Arizona, Minnesota, and South Carolina. While spending most of his time at Notre Dame, Holtz built a record of 216-95-7 over twenty-seven years, including a national championship.

➤ **Pat Riley**—NBA basketball head coach of the Los Angeles Lakers, New York Knicks, and the Miami Heat. During the 1980s with Riley at the helm, the Lakers dominated the league, appearing in the finals seven times in eight years, winning the championship on four of those trips. Additionally,

L.A. won one other championship earlier while Riley was an assistant coach.

➤ **Bill Walsh**—former head coach of the San Francisco 49ers and Stanford University football team. In ten years at the helm, his 49ers won three NFL Super Bowl championships, the first one coming after only three years. Long considered an offensive expert, he won two NFL Coach of the Year awards.

This list is by no means all-inclusive. There are so many other excellent coaches from which to learn.

From all the coaches that I studied, however, I noted many similarities in their coaching methodology that were reflected in my own. Everything begins with the establishment of a well-detailed game plan. And that's when the teaching begins. There is such a strong focus on the preparation of the team in sports, and all the coaches above were, or still are, masters of it. What makes teaching in sports even more definitive is the occurrence of an event from which to learn. Games are used by coaches as the opportunity to reinforce the proper or improper execution of the game plan.

It was obvious that to be a successful coach, you must:

1. Prepare a game plan, based on team strength, that details players' individual roles.

2. Through intense practice, develop the players' abilities, comprehension of their roles, and capability to execute the plan.

3. Allow the players to execute the plan with great discipline at game time.

4. Use past games as opportunities for the team to learn and base all reinforcement on the game plan.

This was typical for so many coaches. In fact, it was how I coached. For myself, it was interesting to note that areas identified as weaknesses for myself as a manager were ones that were strong focuses for me as a coach. As I made notes to myself during my period of self-analysis, I kept noticing that the coaching methodology was fairly well-defined for me. What was most impressive to me, however, was that in sports, the overall game plan permeates every aspect of the team's progression.

What I saw in this approach was present in the methods of some of the legendary coaches that I studied. There is a common methodology to creating a winning team. When I studied the methodology that these other coaches seemed to follow, I found it similar to my own. That's what made me realize that when coaching a sports team, one naturally moves towards this methodology without necessarily determining to do so.

These are the four basic phases in the development of a team. A few years ago, I jotted down these four steps using sports terminology and have referred to them ever since. (More than coincidentally, they are the titles of this book's four sections.) They are:

Step 1: Create and Focus on a Game Plan

Step 2: Develop the Players and their Roles

Step 3: Execute at Game Time

Step 4: Learn From the Game After the Game

The sequence of these steps, obviously, is important. One step cannot happen well until the previous phase has been successfully completed. What is wonderful about this methodology, however, is that it is a dynamic cycle. It can repeat itself in various levels of detail and for an infinite number of times. The only absolute for this approach is that the game plan must be the foundation for it all. Every step of the way, the plan will permeate all activities for a coach and, hopefully, the winning team.

The team's focus will be unified in its direction. Individual actions and group actions will be based on the same premises. The development of the players will be targeted specifically on what is needed for the team's success, since the roles that need to be taught were defined by the plan. Game time actions will be scripted by the methods and individual actions that are itemized in the game plan. And in the end, reviews of the team and player performance will be based on their execution of the game plan's defined assignments.

The Relevance of It All

When I looked at my notes and mulled over my observations, it all became clear to me. There were simple reasons why I was successful as a coach and not as a manager. It was nothing short of a revelation to me. And yet I was embarrassed. Embarrassed by the fact that I could have allowed myself to be so different in the first place, and for not knowing better. But, really, how could I have known? It's not as if anyone ever sat me down and gave me this level of insight. In business today, there isn't always that level of clarity, nor the time to explore it, dwell on it, and absorb it.

When I compared the coaching methodology to the typical management methodology, I found differences in techniques that were obvious to me. For example:

	SUCCESSFUL COACHES	TYPICAL MANAGERS
PLAN	The coach's game plan leads to a team focus that relates the team's objectives to individual roles and predefined performance expectations.	The manager's overall plan leads to quantified goals that usually become the only expectations for employees.
DEVELOP	The most important task for the coach is the development and preparation of the team before the game.	The manager sees himself as most important in the heat of battle because he is the key decision maker.
OBSERVE	The coach can't play the game.	Managers can and do get involved with each employee's work.
LEARN	Coaches review every game with their teams, win or lose, looking for opportunities to reinforce good performance and to correct inappropriate performance.	Managers primarily review performance on an individual basis and often only when it's bad or when required for an annual review.

It was surprising that for two activities that really are very similar, the typical methodology is so very different.

We don't have an easy task as managers. Not only do we have to deliver results, but we also have to worry about employee job satisfaction, workplace harmony, and working collaboratively. The truth is that these latter issues tend to be rather low on the priority list. The nature of business and the need for immediate results tends to drive "softer" issues to the bottom. Understandable, but detrimental.

However, if we can achieve an improvement in the work environment and an increase in employee morale using the same approaches and tactics that will also bring better results, then why not try it? The truth is that it is possible. By trying to create a unified, focused team of individuals who are knowledgeable about their roles and purposes, and who execute well-laid plans and revel in their own successes, we can do just that—get better results while increasing our employees' morale and job satisfaction.

The lessons from my years as a sports coach are laid out in the next four sections. Each lesson, or chapter, is structured in the same manner as my own lessons were: education at the arena, validation of the lesson from the legendary coaches, and the transfer of that lesson into the workplace. At the end of each section, I have included a **Coach's Playbook,** a practical checklist that you can use to help implement these lessons in your organization (the Coach's Playbooks are also consolidated at the end of this book for easy access and use). I hope you'll be able to take these checklists and lessons, which teach valuable techniques and methods, and put them to work building your own winning team.

The Business of Winning

Section 1

Create and Focus on a Game Plan

FAILURE TO PREPARE *is preparing to fail.*

— JOHN WOODEN,
FORMER UCLA BASKETBALL COACH

For any company, sports team, or work group to ever achieve anything, they need to have a plan. Sounds easy. We do it in business all the time. We create business plans, marketing plans, product plans. We think we do a good job of planning. But in the context of a sports team, most of us in the business world don't even rate as planners. In many cases, our plans barely qualify as plans. In fact, when compared to the level of detail included in a sports coach's plans, it becomes obvious that many of us managers barely scratch the surface.

While there may be similarities between sports and business when it comes to creating a purpose and defining goals, there are just as many differences in how individual instructions are detailed out for the people who will be responsible for the execution of the plan. In sports, individual actions are defined in plays that are drawn out, detailed, and rehearsed. The roles that players must follow are comprehended in the plan, not just as individual roles, but rather as one of many roles that must occur simultaneously. A well-coached player is rarely at a loss about what his job is and how he is to contribute to the whole team. That is really where sports plans and business plans differ. If these last few statements concern you, then let's first consider what kind of a plan we're talking about.

If we were to build a plan for a sports team, we would begin on a macro level and end up with well-defined individual details. This comprehensive road map is often referred to as the **game plan.**

The Game Plan Pyramid

A game plan. That's a new term to many business people. In team sports, the term conjures up visions of a team's playbook. But it's much more than just a book of plays to be executed. The game plan encompasses everything that the team is about. It ranges from generic issues, such as a team's overall vision or its playing style, to the specific moves that the players will execute to counter the plays of opposing players in a game. It touches on behavior, motivation, and ambition as much as it deals with executable tasks and actions. It is a catalog of everything that is taught, reinforced, and eventually executed, and it permeates the daily interaction of players, coaches, and staff.

The game plan grows from the top down in a natural progression from an overall purpose to specific details. The process of creating a game plan would flow like this:

> ➤ **Step One:**
> **Vision**
> It begins with the group answering the question:
> **What do we want to achieve?** Any organization
> has to begin with a level of soul-searching philoso-
> phy that defines the group's purpose and vision.

> ➤ **Step Two:**
> **Goals**
> This vision will then take shape as we answer:
> **How will we know when we have achieved it?**
> This results in defined *goals.*

➤ **Step Three:**
Objectives

For each goal that has been defined, we must ask: **How will we achieve it?** The answer will result in quantified *objectives.*

➤ **Step Four:**
Methods/Systems & Style

The plan will then need to link these goals and objectives to the actions of both the entire organization and the individuals. *Methods/Systems* will be identified by answering: **What will we do?** *Style* will be defined by explaining: **In what manner will we do it?**

➤ **Step Five:**
Individual Assignments

The plan eventually will end with a comprehensive blueprint that details the *individual assignments* that are designed to answer the question: **Who will do what in order to deliver the results?**

➤ **Step Six:**
Actions

With no details left to chance, *actions* are developed that can be mastered by individuals in order to define: **What specifically will we do?** This is what is practiced before the game, observed during the game, and critiqued after the game.

➤ **Step Seven:**
Skills, Motivation, Environment &
Team Cooperation

In support of everyone, the coach must have an understanding of: **What will they need to succeed?** This will serve to identify support systems in the areas of *skills, motivation, environment,* and *team cooperation.*

Figure 1. The Game Plan Pyramid

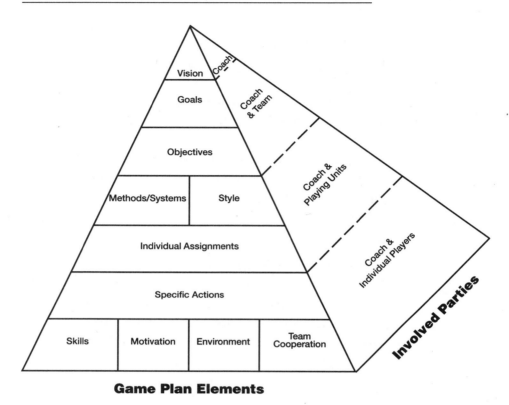

Game Plan Elements

As I sat one day in an empty locker room at the arena, I began to scribble out this relationship between identified goals and specific player instructions. I used the series of questions previously listed, following the process of creating a game plan. On a chalkboard, I started at the top with the vision and worked my way down. In black and white, the diagram in figure 1 became perfectly clear.

As I studied what would become the template for my planning, I realized that with the Rockies, I was using this game plan fully and completely. There was a clear relationship between everything we did and our overall purpose. I could recognize the reason why all of my messages and lessons had common themes. As a coach, it was obvious that preparation, execution, and performance reinforcement should be based on the same plan that evolved out of the team's goals and objectives. And it was all there in the game plans we had created for the Detroit Rockies.

But why worry about having a game plan? Well, when you consider the coach's enormous task with his team, you begin to realize that there are, as they say, a lot of bases to cover. The coach has to shape the mentality of the team, as well as the skills of the players. Therefore, he has to have an overall vision that encompasses all the things associated with his group of players and their tasks. After all, the coach is responsible for defining everything about the team.

But it doesn't all have to be done by the coach alone. Sure, he owns the responsibility for it, and is ultimately accountable for its success or failure. However, defining the game plan is something that often involves players, as well as assistant coaches, even the advice of scouts and sports experts. It can, and should, be a collective effort. In my case, it involved the assistant coaches, as well as the players in limited instances. Involving other parties can only make the game plan stronger and more comprehensive. So on the pyramid, I added the people who might be involved in defining each level.

Now keep in mind that an overall game plan can be expansive if it incorporates all goals, objectives, initiatives, etc. Your overall pyramid may have dozens of different "strains" running down the pyramid—in essence, many smaller pyramids inside of a bigger one. If you include everything you're trying to accomplish, it's going to be big. Of course, many of the low level actions will be the same for different methods, assignments, etc., so it's not as if you're going to create so many different actions at the bottom that it will be unmanageable. Additionally, the pyramid can be used for any event, overall strategy, or challenge. And it can be used at any level of an organization.

So there it was: a powerful model that captured the heart of my coaching methodology and one of the single biggest reasons why I was more successful at the hockey arena than at work.

The best thing about this template was that it was completely ready for me to use at work. All I had to do was fill in the blanks.

Laying the Groundwork

Creating the game plan and focusing the players on it will be the coach's first step towards success. If this phase is completed well, the result will be a team's clarity of purpose and focus. Furthermore, it will be obvious to team members what their roles will be in creating a total team effort. For the coach, the first task will be to **build the game plan**. The game plan will need to include everything from overall vision to specific support needs. In order to chart a course towards a championship, the coach and players should first understand that it is important to **define your destination**.

With that understanding, the game plan begins to add details for execution. Any organization will have strengths and weaknesses, so it is important to tailor the plan to **use any unique attributes you have**. Any successful plan will need to take into account the current capabilities and strengths of the team. Additionally, the plan will be easier to execute if the manner in which players will be expected to execute their assignments takes into account their natural tendencies. For that reason, it's critical to **develop your playing style based upon your players**. Once the plan is defined it needs to be communicated to the players so that they not only comprehend but internalize the detailed roles. A coach must strive to create a thorough game plan with the team that generates confidence in its chances for success.

Like any CEO or army general, a coach can never forget that **players want to believe in their coaches**. That loyalty and trust will come from the acceptance and ownership of the plan by each team member. Unfortunately, a coach will need to be prepared for the ocassions where a player does not accept or cannot execute their roles. In an effort to protect the overall team, the coach must remember that **if a player doesn't fit with the game plan, get rid of the player**.

CHAPTER 1

Build the Game Plan

*IF YOU WANT TO GET SOMETHING DONE,
you can't have a bunch of alternatives. You have
to have absolutes.*

— MIKE KRZYZEWSKI
BASKETBALL COACH, DUKE UNIVERSITY

THE COACH'S LESSON

When I was building my hockey team, I had crudely drafted what would become our overall game plan. This was in the form of many pages of notes that seemed unrelated. Our overall goal, in the short term, was to be competitive with the best teams, and in the long term, to win everything. That became our *vision*. We knew we weren't going to win any championships in those first years. In fact, we knew we'd lose enough games to make us numb. It would be enough for us to be able to compete with the best.

Of the many *goals* that we would have to reach in order to be competitive, one of the most important was to reduce the goals scored against us. There was no way in hell that we could survive playing some of the superior teams if we continued to get down by four or six goals during the game. If we could lower the number of goals scored against us, or the "goals against average per game," we could settle into our game plan, instead of frantically trying to perform miracles.

For us to lower the number of goals scored against us, we would need to reduce the number of shots opponents took against us (we wanted it below thirty). This was much easier said than done! For us, the real problems came from our inability to handle rebounds around our net, and the fact that we couldn't clear the puck out of our end zone. Their players would take three or four shots at our goalie, while we tried to follow the puck like mad lemmings. We had to minimize their chances around our net on rebounds. This became one of our *objectives* that, if achieved, would help us meet our overall goal.

Now, up until this point, I had only identified our future state. Where were we trying to go? By laying out a vision and quantifying the performance levels necessary to get there, I had clearly established what we had to become. "Now if that's where we need to go," I asked myself, "how are we going to get there?"

For a sports team, this is a natural point in the development of the plan. The coach has to identify both the methods and the style for the team. In other words, "What will we do?" and "In what way will we do it?" At this point, my analysis turned to what we were. I looked at our team, evaluating our strengths and weaknesses, and tried to identify our capabilities. What could we be capable of doing and in what fashion could we do it?

Referring back to the objective of reducing shots on our net in order to reduce goals scored against us, I began to itemize our approach. We would employ a few *methods and systems* that, if executed, would satisfy our objectives. One of these was a defensive zone positioning scheme that would put our players in critical areas. This scheme would give us continuous defensive presence in front of our own net, something we needed if we were going to reduce the number of rebounds the other team was allowed to get. With our defensemen protecting the net, our left and right wingers would stay away from the net in areas around the other team's defensemen. The positioning of our forwards would greatly reduce the number of shots that the opposing defensemen were allowed to take, as well as put two of our players in a good position to break out of our end with the puck if and when we got control of it. This positional scheme would give us some much-needed relief in our end, if we could execute the details.

At this stage, early in the planning process, the team's *style* starts to take shape. This helps to define the manner in which the team will execute all that they will do. I looked at how we normally played and compared it to what would be required to support the methods and systems we had identified. We could play a well-structured game plan that was supported by plenty of self-control by the players. It would be a stretch for some of the guys, but self-control was within their grasp. On defense, we would be disciplined, with an emphasis on control and structure. Discipline to our positions! Discipline to our assignments! Discipline to our individual tasks!

In this defensive format, there would be many *individual assignments*, depending on the different situations. For our two defensemen, their one basic assignment would be to always "maintain possession of our net." Their primary role was to physically tie up any opponent in front of our goalie. Only one of them would be in front of the net at any given time, however, allowing his partner to battle for control of the puck in the corners. If the puck moved to the other side of the ice, they would switch roles. In front of the net, they would have to "box out" opposing players when rebounds occurred, using their physical abilities to move opponents without drawing penalties.

To do this, they would have to execute *specific actions*. These elements of the game plan were distinct to each player and each situation. For example, our defensemen in front of our net would need to do such chores as pushing other players using only upper body muscles and their stick. Therefore, our defensemen needed to learn good posture and form to utilize their strength best without losing their balance.

Below all of that, we would need to build a solid foundation of support. We would have to teach good *skills* to assure correct execution. These would only be defined by the identified tasks: a true needs-driven approach. These skills would be clear, understandable acts, motions, or thoughts that could be taught or developed. For our defensemen in front of the net, they would be practiced motions such as using lower body posturing for upper body leverage during a physical check.

I identified *motivation* sources for inspiration and encouragement of the team, playing units, and individuals. It's essential for a coach to know what "buttons" to push. Every player, every small group, every team has a reaction to some sort of motivation. It will vary for individuals and with different situations. For my hockey team, the fact that we were the only all-black team around inspired them. As individuals, they were all different. Damien loved to know that he was improving. Corey loved to be treated like a leader. For our defensemen, I challenged them to protect the net as their own personal property being attacked by outsiders. Soon they were bragging about keeping people out of their "house."

The team needed an *environment* that encouraged all of them to focus on learning, developing, and contributing. Our team needed good ice to practice on and plenty of time on it, as well as high-quality hockey equipment. (That wasn't easy since a hockey stick can cost $30 and an hour of ice $130.) However, thanks to some great parents and guardians, the players never had to worry about these details.

My biggest task would be to establish the *team cooperation* that drives all players to work together for the good of the whole team. Beyond games, this needs to be founded and built on team unity, camaraderie, and respect for each other as people. On the ice during games, however, it can only come from an understanding of every other player's responsibility. The Rockies were a family first, so the camaraderie and personal care was already there. What had to come was the comprehension of each other's roles and responsibilities. For our defensemen protecting the front of our net, this challenged them even more. They had to know where our forwards would be without looking so that a quick turnover of the puck by the other team could be capitalized upon immediately. If we were to look at this small portion of the game plan and put it into the pyramid form, it might look like figure 2.

The game plan became the all-inclusive guide to all of our actions and behaviors. The game plan was always reinforced—and repeated again and again. There was always consistency in my messages, my lessons, and my reinforcement. I had to deliver the same message, the same lessons, and the same reinforcements of the same behaviors. With that level of detail in the game plan, there is an established relationship between the team's overall purpose and the minutiae closest to the players. It is comprehensive. And it is a powerful tool for a coach.

The Game Plan Provides the Focus

This game plan, once created, will become the foundation for all activities. When players' roles are created, they will be based on the game plan.

Figure 2. The Game Plan Pyramid—Detroit Rockies Style

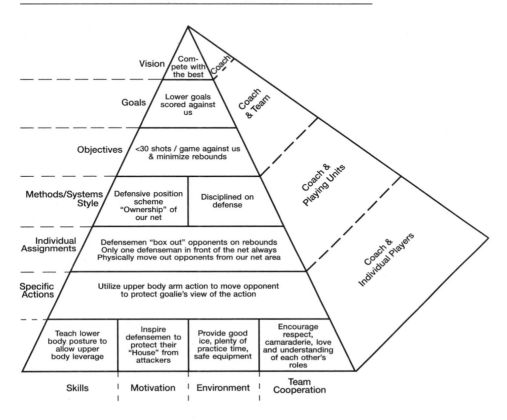

When lessons are taught, they will be derived from the plan. During the games, the players will execute the plan. After the game, when there are opportunities to learn from, measure, and reinforce performances, their performances will be measured against the game plan. For me, it certainly became the center of my coaching activity.

In sports, I had often read about or heard of the development of game plans. It always amazed me that there was a science to it all—the evolution from an overall strategy to the eventual definition of specific acts. When I studied some of the legendary coaches, I saw a similar adherence to this format. They all built a strong relationship between individual player actions and the overall mission of the team. It all became incredibly clear to me as I learned about one of the most famous plays in all of professional football.

Lesson from a Legend: The Lombardi Sweep

Perhaps no other play in all of sports shows the relationship of an overall team mission to the explicit roles and actions of individuals than the Sweep that made the Green Bay Packers famous during their NFL glory days in the 1960s. It is the single play that took the image of Vince Lombardi beyond that of just another coach to, instead, one of the greatest sports minds of all time. He is a legend in the NFL and beyond. His name is immortalized on the league's championship prize: the Vince Lombardi Trophy, more commonly referred to as the Super Bowl trophy.

When Lombardi took over a floundering Green Bay squad, the overall *vision* was to create a championship team; nothing less than that would do. While developing their game plan, Lombardi went back to basics. Realizing that the team needed to build a solid foundation on which it could always rely, he drew on his earlier lessons in life.

Lombardi believed in the Jesuit philosophy of "freedom through discipline and simplicity." This would become one of the overall *goals* of his game plan. He took over a Packers playbook that was measured in inches thick and reduced it to pages. Instead of having many different plays and formations with only a few options to them, he maintained only a handful of plays and formations, but with many different options.

Being a former offensive lineman himself, Lombardi focused first on his offensive unit. His goal was to have a group of eleven men who could handle all kinds of adversity and challenge on the playing field. He wanted his players to be able to adjust to whatever formation or movement they saw from their defensive opponents. To achieve this, Lombardi knew that the Packers had to have one play that would define them. If they could accomplish this *objective,* the Packers' offensive unit could become totally responsive to any situation presented to it at any time. It could render any defensive game plan or adjustment ineffective.

For Lombardi, it was play 49: the Packer Sweep, later to be referred to as the Lombardi Sweep. This was their lead play. In Lombardi's own words he suggested, "every team arrives at a lead play… a bread and butter play. It is the play that the team knows it must make go and the one that opponents know they must stop. Continued success with it, of course, makes a No. 1 play because from that success stems your own team's confidence." The play became an overall *system*. More than just a single play, it had multiple options, allowing players the flexibility to adapt their movements to whatever they encountered.

Lombardi wanted his Packers to dominate. He wanted them to settle for nothing short of their best performance. Their *style* of play was marked by their relentless pursuit of perfection. Mistakes were not tolerated. And nothing short of complete, personal dedication, commitment, and sacrifice to the team would be allowed. This was evident in their games, practices, meetings, film reviews, even in the way they dressed.

With this doctrine, Lombardi defined for the players their roles in the Sweep.

The coach drew on the board every detail of every player in every conceivable situation reacting to every possible opponent's movement. Each player was taught, not simply how to react to each situation, but why he should react in that manner. With this level of definition, each player's role brought with it definite *individual assignments*. The center, for example, had the important assignment of protecting the backfield while the offensive guard, one of the most important players on the Sweep, pulled out of his position to run around the line and block for the running back.

For the Packers, these assignments then defined the specific *actions* to be used. The center had specific tasks to perform to accomplish his assignment. After snapping the football, he had to step quickly to his right in order to hook the charging defensive tackle to the left. This block would force the defensive tackle to the opposite side, into traffic, thus keeping him from entering the backfield where the running back was taking the hand-off.

For the offensive center to successfully neutralize the opposing tackle, the hook block had to be executed precisely. This specific block required *skills* to be mastered that would lead to a quick motion, with a turn correctly timed and the delivery of a well-leveraged block. During practices, for hours, movements such as these would be repeated over and over.

As a source of *motivation* for players, Lombardi used the Sweep as a personal statement for his offensive linemen. He wanted them to treat this single play as the definition of their Green Bay squad. For the offensive line especially, the Sweep defined them as a playing unit. It had to be executed with confident pride. And it could not fail.

To this end, the Packers practiced this play for countless hours. Lombardi created an *environment* where commitment to excellence and intensity in preparation was mandatory. He totally changed the décor of the offices. He created a separate room for viewing game films. He positioned cars in the parking lot so that their headlights could be used to illuminate the practice field late at night. He made his offense run the Packers Sweep over and over again. Many players recall that, for weeks on end, it seemed as if the Sweep was the only play they ever practiced. So accurate were their movements that their initial stances were measured, practiced, and, eventually, became instinctual. Lombardi could sense if the tight end was in his usual position of only eight feet away from the offensive tackle, instead of the nine feet that the Sweep required.

The Sweep, when properly executed, became a synchronous display of movements that personified *team cooperation*. By paying careful attention to every player's role and teaching the entire team all of those roles, Lombardi achieved his goal of creating a group of men who were completely unified in their thinking. Players had to know exactly where their teammates were in order to avoid collisions as they shifted positions midplay.

As a part of their overall game plan, the relationship between the team's overall goals and the minutiae of the individuals' tasks were constantly reinforced.

If we were to put this into the game plan pyramid, it might look like figure 3.

Figure 3. The Game Plan Pyramid—Lombardi Sweep

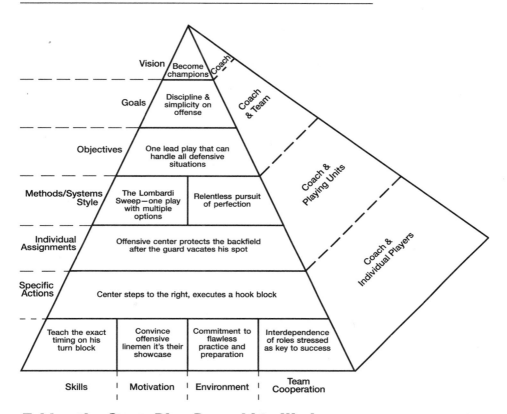

Taking the Game Plan Pyramid to Work

When comparing my role as a team coach to my job as a manager, I made a number of observations that only highlighted the importance of a good game plan. I realized that I hadn't established a firm relationship between our overall goals and the specific actions required. The team at work didn't have a clear vision of how the details mattered, or even why. And I, as a manager, had no consistency to my daily reinforcement of their actions. Instead, I was only encouraging their haphazard behavior by varying my recognition of behaviors based on such scientific methods as my mood or the decibels of my boss' voice. We, as a team, lacked a clear focus of our destination as well as the road map and driving instructions to get us there.

I took my notes from the arena to work and began trying to fill in the blanks. This was not going to be as easy as it was in the arena. Coaches seem to gravitate to this method, since the need to draw out specific plays is inherent to the coaching role. Managing, however, is 180 degrees away from that. At least it was for me. Nobody prepared me to approach managing a work group as a team. The farthest thing from my mind was having to specifically "draw out plays" with them. "These are professionals," I thought. "They know what their job is." But the fact is, just as the professional coach has to define roles and draw out plays with his or her players, so does the manager in business.

So I took a shot at it. I picked one particular aspect of our overall business plan and tried to apply it. Our division had recently come out with a set of common measurements for all manufacturing sites. These measurements consisted of nineteen different charts measuring key performance indicators. I recall thinking that it was a terrific move by top leadership to establish some common measures, as well as to clarify the targets. I took these measures and began to list them in the game plan pyramid I had brought from the arena. As could be expected, they fit perfectly.

> **Vision:** Our overall vision was to be a world-class manufacturer in every measure.

> **Goals:** Our goals were defined by the nineteen measurements.

> **Objectives:** For each of our goals, there were specific, quantified objectives. They defined specific deliverable targets that could be related directly to our overall vision. It was perfect. And that's where it stopped.

I tried to follow the pyramid down, but I couldn't. I realized that for all the terrific definition there was for the goals and objectives, there was none that related to the actions of individuals. I looked at it and began to think about how I was managing. It seems that too often, we take the vision, the goals, and the objectives, and communicate them all to the organization. And then with the proverbial pat on the rump, we say "Now go get 'em." For my group, there didn't seem to be enough details for the employees. Oh sure, I had some different systems and a few initiatives to begin implementing, and perhaps a sound practice or two. And, of course, people had their job assignments defined for them. But realistically, I hadn't "drawn out any plays" with my work team. There were no "drills and practices" to ensure proper execution. And there definitely lacked any clear, consistent reinforcement of their behaviors that related back to the overall plan.

PUTTING THE LESSON IN ACTION

In the sports environment, a coach must work with players to fill in the detail. Designed plays cannot succeed without that level of definition. In the workplace, however, it's not so obvious to managers. Many don't think to add that detail. Nor do they recognize that failures can be traced back to the absence of those particulars.

Additionally, I had never considered using my work team to help create this game plan. I had always believed that their objectives, methods, assignments, etc. would have to be developed by me alone. The reality that I learned in the arenas of sports showed me otherwise. While the top levels of the pyramid may be up to the coach alone, the players often know enough to participate in creating the details for the lower levels. It is up to the coach to ensure that the game plan is well-constructed and thorough. However, the coach can involve the entire team in putting all the details together. The fact is that if players are involved in a sports team's development, they will buy into it, believe in it, and be more positive about executing it. The same goes for the workplace team. If they are involved in developing the vision or defining their quantified goals and objectives, they will internalize the plan from the beginning. So, as I moved forward with our game plan at work, I involved the whole group, leaving only the direction of the overall exercise as my unique assignment.

And so I forced us to fill in the blanks of our game plan. It took a number of weeks just to identify all that was absent. Over the course of the next few months, I developed a much better understanding of what was both missing and needed. Our approach followed the same path as that of my hockey team: "where are we going?" versus "where are we right now?"

Vision

The vision at the top of our pyramid, along with the goals and objectives, helped to define what our future state had to be. Those had already been well-established. Our vision was to become a world-class manufacturer.

Goals

One specific goal was to build all products right the first time.

Objectives

In support of that goal, one of the quantified objectives for our process was to have no less than 95 percent First Time Quality on any given shift of production. What was lacking was the definition of what we were going to do to get there and in what manner we would do it.

So before defining either methods or style, we looked at our present day reality. We had capabilities, strengths, and weaknesses, just like any group. But what stood out most of all was the amount of talent that we had and the quickness with which team members could accomplish their own tasks and assignments. That speed, leveraged with their knowledge and ability, had to be capitalized upon to help us move quickly as a group.

Style

Our style would have to be one that was quick to react, but always relying on data so that we would be prepared to make quick decisions without compromising the quality of those decisions.

Methods/Systems

That eventually led to the identification of methods and systems that we would employ. The quality goals for reducing repairs on our assembly lines had a whole list of particular initiatives underneath it. One of them was a corporate-wide initiative to reduce and eliminate sources of manufacturing errors. This method would utilize statistical tracking of repair activity and a unique engineering approach to problem solving.

Individual Assignments

The methods and systems then further defined the roles for all of the team members. It did much more than our simple employee job descriptions. Within these defined roles, there were specific executable assignments. That kind of detail was **not** listed on job descriptions. For example, the new process for statistically tracking repair activity would require everyone to react in different manners. There would be daily involvement by the operations management folks for problems that were abnormal and unpredictable, while engineering focused on long-term solutions to chronic problems that were predictable.

Actions

The assignments came to life for my team members as their specific actions were structured. To support our new repair tracking and improvement process, we would need to develop good habits, utilizing sound statistical practices, while developing tools to monitor regularly both short- and long-term activities. The production department would need to closely monitor all activity in repair areas by establishing a real-time, orchestrated response, on the hour, to any repairs. Engineering, on the other hand, would need to employ detailed problem solving tools and methods to eliminate permanently the causes of our top defects.

Skills

We needed to teach skills to these groups in order to support them in their assignments. The engineering groups received training in a new problem solving approach that assessed the risks inherent in a process before it was ever implemented, aiming to eliminate problems before they were created.

Motivation

Our motivation depended on two ultimate "must-haves." We absolutely had to build a product that both we and our customers would be proud of, and we had to be the best among manufacturers in GM. Our customers and our leadership had to be satisfied, and nothing short of that could be allowed. I had a young, aggressive group of workers who were all looking for opportunities to impress, and I capitalized upon it. I stressed the fact that our customers were depending on us and our higher management was concentrating on our customer satisfaction measurements. That focused both the conscientious and the self-centered people on one common measurement: customer satisfaction. Our desire to be the best fit well with the urge to boast about it when we were.

Environment

To be able to act quickly and decisively on a real-time basis, we would need an environment that was conducive to timely response. We needed to have information, updated daily and presented to us in a clear, concise manner that made our tasks visually obvious. To this end, we created boards that displayed all the data, charts, action plans, and history that we needed at our fingertips. We posted these in the workplace at the source of the repairs.

Team Cooperation

In what was the biggest change from the way we operated, the team came to understand team cooperation. There could be no success without the entire team coming together. Wanting to act that way and saying that we wanted to act that way was **not** new for us. However, defining actions that would drive team cooperation, discussing every member's role with the entire group, and teaching the team specifics to help them understand the tasks of others was new. In recognition of how important this aspect of team interaction was, I set out to identify specific actions, such as encouraging open dialogue through increased roundtable discussions, improving personal relationships by organizing after-work social activities, and bringing issues or decisions to closure through group consensus whenever feasible, that would help to increase team cooperation.

After our own game plan had matured to this level, I tried to scribble the detail into the pyramid and soon found that I hadn't left enough room at the bottom. I realized that while there was too much detail for the bottom of my diagram, there would not be too much detail for the bottom of my organization. That's exactly where we needed the most details.

Of course, there are so many details that were part of the plan. This is only one strain of it. So, an abbreviated example of my own game plan would look like figure 4.

Figure 4. The Game Plan Pyramid—In the Workplace

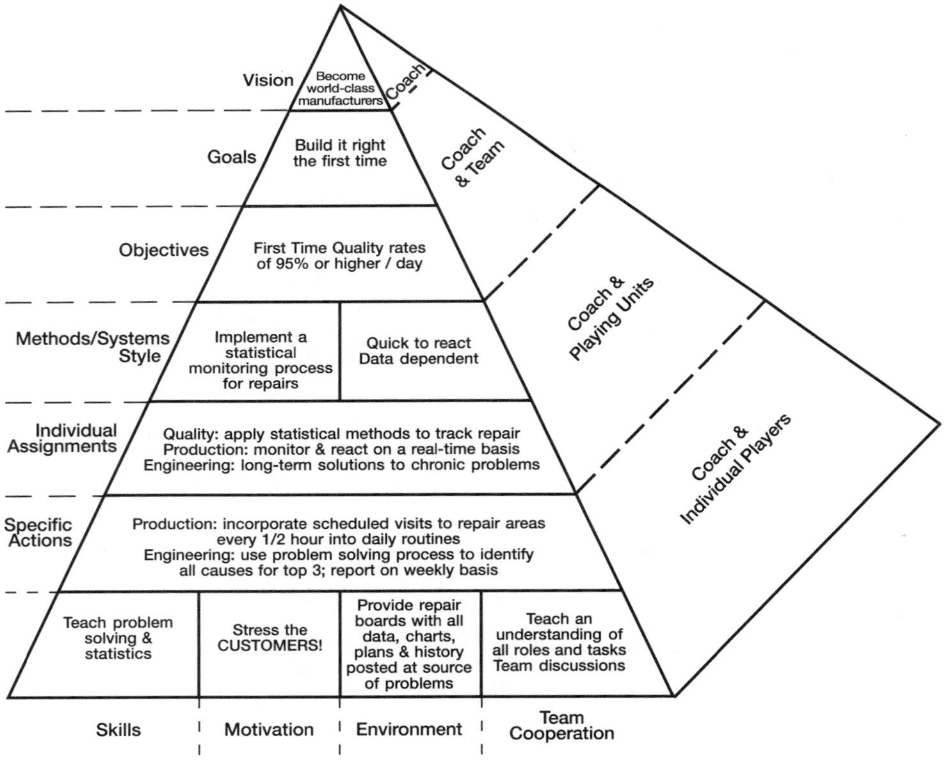

Once I felt comfortable with this approach in the workplace, I began talking in this context when leading meetings of my management team. I talked about the relationship between individual tasks and behaviors and our overall vision. I referred to the methods and systems as the means to the end in our quest to meet all of our targets. When reinforcing behavior, good or bad, I referred to our overall plan and the relationships that defined it.

After using this method for a while, our organization developed a much better focus. Our actions became more efficient, since there was little that we did that wasn't keenly directed to our overall objectives. In fact, we began to use our overall game plan to rationalize ending past practices or scratching ongoing projects that were not in line with our plan.

The game plan didn't solve all of our problems. That was up to us. But it did provide some much needed clarity and purpose to our actions. That alone made our days much more meaningful.

CHAPTER 2

Define Your Destination

NEVER LOOK WHERE YOU'RE GOING. Always look where you want to go.

— BOB ERNST
ROWING COACH, UNIVERSITY OF WASHINGTON

THE COACH'S LESSON

The Detroit Rockies were getting ready to move into their last year at the Bantam age level, (roughly 12–14 years old). The team had mediocre success the previous season and was expecting to fare much better in the coming season. I decided early on to set my sights high with the hockey team. I knew that the odds were stacked against us, so I decided that I wanted to best prepare them to play at the highest level of competition. After talking it over with my assistant coaches, George and Alex, we all agreed that we should move the team up to the Midget age level one year early, in order to spend three full years playing at that level. The age of the boys allowed us to do that, and the fear of losing wasn't going to keep us away from the valuable lessons we could gain at a higher level.

The parents of the Rockies' players thought we were crazy to move the team up to a higher level. They considered this move somewhat premature.

The competition was much stronger, faster, and on average, two to three years older. I knew the team would suffer through some humiliating defeats, but I convinced the kids that one day they would win at that level. During the first twenty games or so, it was tough to keep the boys emotionally in the games. Often, they felt defeated even before the games started. Expecting to lose and keeping an open mind to learning doesn't take away the sting of losing. Some of the players questioned what was going on. They asked, "Why bother trying?" Many of them contemplated quitting. Throughout all of this, it was important to keep the locker room positive. It was obvious to me that I needed them to share my vision.

That's when I decided to involve them in a visualization exercise. "When you were younger and you got your first two-wheel bicycle, what did you dream of doing with it?" I asked them. Answers ranged from racing other boys and touring the city to jumping over buses.

Then I asked, "Now what happened the first time you went riding that same bike without the training wheels on it?" Sure enough, they all claimed to have fallen down—a lot. "So did you give up riding? Or did you keep at it because you still wanted to jump over buses?" I followed that with examples relating to skating on ice for the first time and finally made the point that if your goals are set high, you will probably fail in the early going—but that's okay. That's to be expected and it is part of the process. But you never give up because you always keep your vision in mind.

I began reinforcing the fact that there was a long-term plan that would require us to make sacrifices in the short-term. I reminded them of that during games, in practices, and in the dressing room. I tried to keep practices positive and loose, allowing them to have fun. Discussions and lessons were always framed by the talk of "how awesome we're going to be when we master these lessons." I relied on the individual team members who remained positive and optimistic to encourage some of the players who were down. I talked to some of the more influential parents, convincing them of what I saw as necessary developmental experiences for the boys, and asked for their support.

During this period, I helped them identify the aspects of the superior opponent's play that we wanted to emulate. We tried to keep focused on what other teams were doing well that we would have to learn, such as the way they used their defensemen during a power play, or their work in front of our net. This helped to identify where we wanted to be in a year or two.

We set development goals to work on in the short term, usually one aspect at a time. When we observed teams that had a terrific power play and passed the puck well, I engaged the boys in conversation after the games. "Wow, they sure moved that puck well on their power play, didn't they?"

They would marvel, "We couldn't touch them." With that recognition, our conversation would end with the agreed upon need to improve their own puck handling skills, develop better passing techniques, and maintain their composure under pressure. Watching other players on the ice helped the Rockies identify specifically what each player would have to do to strengthen our team play and help us win games at that level.

The most important aspect of this exercise was that we did it together. I remember one game that the Rockies lost to a team whose captain was a terrific, unselfish player. He was so impressive that some of the boys were commenting on his play in the dressing room afterwards. The tone of their discussion made it apparent that inside each of them, they longed to be that good. Stopping the conversation in order to engage the entire team in the discussion, I asked players to name what they thought was so impressive about that particular athlete's play. They began to list characteristics. They described some of his good moves and excellent passes. We centered the discussion around his strongest skill: passing. At that point, the conversation became introspective. "Why don't we pass like that?" was one of the self-directed questions. From that point, their answers to my questions seemed to all follow the same path, "We should do…." Not only did they understand that they had to improve, but they helped to determine how and where they had to change.

So we continued to lose games. The difference was that there seemed to be a purpose to our losing. We were gaining two important qualities: knowledge of our own game, and the resolve to improve it. As ludicrous as the hope of winning sounded after losing games by fifteen goals, the team's hunger to win at a higher level was strong. We were focused and determined early in the season. We knew what would be required to become a winning team. Of course, that didn't make the road any easier to walk, or, rather, skate. Many of them realized that since the coaches were committed to the long haul, that there must be better days ahead. And indeed there were.

The Difference Between Winning and Just Surviving

Successful coaches make no mistake about who the competition is. There is a big difference between "wanting to be able to compete" and "wanting to be the competition." It is what differentiates a winning attitude from a survivalist one.

Often, when a new professional coach is hired, the media does much to anticipate and publicize the coach's plans. The desire and vision of the new leader gets a great deal of attention early on. Some people are surprised to hear the new coach of a struggling, last place team talking about competing for the championship. Critics are quick to challenge that line of thinking as unrealistic. "Surely he can't be serious," they often say.

As impractical as this championship talk may sound at the time, there is no better time for a coach to establish a winning attitude than on day one. These are coaches that understand the power of setting ambitious goals. Players want to know that the coach has the same purpose. Players, who all too often are faced with the mortality of their careers, also want to know that their coach's desire is as ambitious as their own. While coaches *do* want to win, saying so publicly can be part of a calculated effort to rev up the players.

It cannot be overstressed that the visualization of a future state must be shared with the team members. Players must "own" the vision, agreeing in their desire for it and believing that it's possible. While they may not be involved by the coach in setting the overall vision, goals, or even objectives, they must internalize them. This necessitates the coach spending time sharing these with the players in a way that brings the possibilities to life. Coaches may use visualization exercises and hypothetical discussion that ask "What do you think it will be like when we are finally able to...." Others may ask players to develop their own answers to compare against what has already been defined. Regardless of method, if the coach can turn the players into believers, then the development can begin.

Of course, there should be no false conception that there will be some magical consensus reached throughout this. It may not be possible to get all players to believe, let alone agree. That should not deter the exercise or the attempt to get as many players as possible on board the attitude train before it leaves the station. Detractors normally exist on all teams. The coach's main concern should be to galvanize enough support from a critical mass to jump-start the learning cycle.

This first step—creating the top levels of the pyramid—may be one of the most important in creating the game plan, since it defines the direction, pace, and ultimate feedback for all that the team will do. Everything that cascades through the game plan down to the players will be aimed at this high point. It must be well-defined, clear, and understood by all. There should be left no questions in the minds of players as to what the ultimate purpose is.

Lesson from a Legend: Vince Lombardi

 In 1959, Vince Lombardi accepted the head coaching job of the NFL's Green Bay Packers. With much fanfare, he took the helm of a team that had just finished a horrible 1-10-1 season. In fact, the Packers' losing ways had made a mockery of football in Wisconsin as they managed to lose more than *twice* as many games as they had won in the 1950s. Lombardi had no intentions of continuing that bad habit. While being photographed as he left for Wisconsin, Lombardi was asked by a reporter about taking on a losing team. He replied, "I have never been associated with a loser, and I don't expect to be now."

Upon arriving at the Green Bay Packers' team offices, he immediately gave the building a makeover. He called the offices "a disgrace" and went about destroying any visual reminders of a losing organization. Gone was the worn out furniture, drab pictures, and peeling paint on the walls. It was replaced by a new professional look that included new wallpaper on walls, accompanied by fresh furniture and decorations. Startled staff members could only look on in disbelief as their environment was torn apart.

The look and feel of the office décor was less important than the message Lombardi was delivering. "We're not just going to start with a clean slate," he said, "we're going to throw the old slate away." From day one, Lombardi let the Packers know that they were going to settle for nothing less than success.

The Coach as Manager: Setting Ambitious Goals

For people to accept change, they must first accept the notion that they need to change. This is true for the living, breathing entity that is any organization. If a manager promptly focuses the group on a vision that is ambitious, then the need to change should be an inescapable conclusion. When group members begin to assess their shortcomings in the context of their challenges, they can then help define what and how they need to change.

Like the sports coach, the manager must create the top layers of the game plan pyramid for the work group. An ambitious vision must be defined by goals and quantified objectives that are both meaningful and challenging. And the members of the work team must be brought to the same level of buy-in that the sports players are. They must internalize and personalize the vision, while becoming focused on the quantified objectives. For this reason, the manager will need to spend an ample amount of time communicating and discussing these top levels with all employees.

There is no excuse for setting less than ambitious goals for the organization. It is true that objectives must be based on some degree of realism and attainability; however, the end result cannot be anything less than ultimately winning. There must always exist a challenge that will push the organization to become something it is not.

Just as a high jumper knows exactly how high the bar is before he attempts to jump, so too must the work group know its goal. The goal must be quantified. That will help to better define the challenge. Performance measurements should be in place in order to constantly keep score of progress. Gauging a team's progress is important in order to reinforce the overall plan. There should never be any secret about the gap between current results and desired results. The game plan loses functionality if it does not gain detail as the vision cascades down the pyramid.

If the goals are set ambitiously, then it will be easy for some doubtful people to become frustrated or disillusioned by what might seem to be impossible tasks. That should be expected. Here a manager needs to bring the group back to the overall plan in place to achieve it. The manager needs to stress to the group that their diligence in working the game plan will pay off eventually. All members of the team should be able to tell when they have reached their goals. Quantified milestones will help them identify progress. Additionally, all employees should be able to envision how the achievement of the goals will help them individually. It might be a financial incentive, an easier workday, or perhaps stronger job security. Whatever the incentive is, if the team members can see the end result of all of their hard work, they may be encouraged to persevere.

Keep in mind that an aggressive goal is meant to inspire people, not to defeat them. If you set a goal that is *too* high to be attained, the team suffers failure and the morale problems that go along with it. Contrarily, if the goal is too low that only minor improvements on current performance are required to meet it, the reward of reaching the goal won't seem that great. The most difficult part of goal setting is finding that place in between that presents an ambitious, yet attainable, goal. Goals must balance the need to achieve maximum benefit for the organization, while not overtaxing the capabilities of those within the organization. The vision of tomorrow must be perceived within the context of the reality of today.

Effective Goal Setting Exercises

There are four ingredients that must go into an effective goal setting exercise:

➤ An understanding of customer requirements.

➤ A thorough analysis of the competition's performance.

➤ An aggressive assessment of the organization's capabilities.

➤ The involvement of the people who will be expected to achieve the goal.

The manager must consider these four factors to create an aggressive, yet achievable goal. A brokerage house that is considering customers' demands for 24-hour customer service will have to balance that requirement against what competitors are offering (e.g. full service vs. automated service), what the organization is capable of supporting (e.g. time, money, and resources), and the employees' ideas on executing the plan (e.g. hire additional staff, go online). The outcome will be a plan that will be:

➤ Aggressively based on what customers want.

➤ Poised to challenge competitors.

➤ Capable of being supported.

➤ Achievable, as determined by employees.

The more aggressive a goal is, the more difficult it will be to maintain employee enthusiasm towards achieving it. Many management styles will tell you to set goals extraordinarily high, hoping only to achieve 80 percent of the goal, which is really all you want to achieve anyway. This sets employees up to chase the proverbial carrot that remains always out of reach. This approach assumes that employees will not realize that the manager is playing them as fools. This is not a good relationship to establish between management and employees. In fact, it can be quite destructive if ever discovered by those who have been duped. It's better to maintain credibility with goals.

Stay Positive

It's important to keep a positive spin on the overall objective. Success is a more powerful motivator than failure. The hard knocks taken along the way need to be interpreted as necessary and purposeful. This is especially true if a group is indeed improving, either by incremental gains towards objectives, or by gaining knowledge and experience that will make it better in the end. If the lack of success can be kept in the context of a learning, developing organization, then people will see that progress is being made and that the failures are serving a purpose. This will only help to train them to become winners. If they are learning about their own game play and are determined to improve it and willing to work at it, then you are losing with a purpose. The knowledge that progress is being made can help to reinforce the development process for a team. It's important for a manager to bring the team's attention, if only momentarily, to any reassuring aspect of their work. Losing while feeling down can only deflate a team. Conversely, losing while looking up can serve to make a group more resolute.

PUTTING THE LESSON IN ACTION

While managing a large assembly operation, my team and I received what seemed to be an insurmountable challenge from higher management. We were to average more than 90 percent to gross capacity for a month on a large automotive assembly line that had never averaged more than 63 percent. We had one year to get there. It was a carrot, and I knew it. While I understood the need to achieve this goal, I privately knew that I would not be betting my paycheck on our attainment of the goal.

Members of my management team met my communication with laughter. "Where's the bottle of magic foo-foo dust that we're going to sprinkle on this operation?" one asked amid the group's laughter. Another suggested that we should also solve world hunger and try to invent a time machine, too. The fact remained that we weren't even close to our goal. Yet, while everyone shook their heads in disbelief, the "90 percent in twelve months" challenge became our goal.

I recognized that my leaders had given me the "top of the pyramid." They had defined the vision, the goals, and the objectives. In some areas, they had even presented us with ideas for the methods and systems to achieve those objectives. What I didn't have was the bottom of the pyramid. The "how" was missing; the "what will people do" was absent; the "what support will be needed for them to succeed" was AWOL. Just as I did with the Rockies, I began to fill in the details of the game plan.

We started with dissecting our operation. It didn't take long before I realized that we needed to define our style, before we went much further. I decided to involve the team in this exercise. With an open mind, we visualized the future state that we desired. We began to talk about what it would be like if we ran at that level of performance. "How would we act? What would we accept and what would we refuse to tolerate? How would we treat our equipment? What would our acceptance of quality defects be?" we asked each other. We would visualize how we had to operate both individually and as an organization.

Moving on to more details, we analyzed all the data we could find to highlight problems that we weren't seeing. It was important for us to understand all of our shortcomings. We needed to challenge ourselves. We had to throw out the status quo and start to think aggressively. Our current methods and practices were questioned, while new ones were suggested. It was in this new, "anything goes" thinking environment that we began to discover what needed to change if our results were ever going to change.

We also visited and studied other manufacturing facilities that were running well. It all served to help us identify the areas where we would need to improve. After recognizing the differences between our present and our future states, we created the plans that would help to bridge that gap. We all understood that we were aiming for a level of performance that was incredibly aggressive and would be close to world class.

What was amazing to watch was how a group of people become more creative and resourceful when faced with a significant challenge. This was especially true when it involved goals that they wanted to meet. Our plans became lengthier than ever before. There was more detail. There were more contingencies. They were aggressive in their timing. We knew that what we wanted to be would require us to act differently than before.

I remember a moment when, after reviewing our plans, I sensed a feeling among the group: "We can do it."

And then we put our plan into motion. Step by step, we inched forward, but the progress came slowly. There were failures and less than stellar success. Unfortunately, our top leadership didn't always have the patience for our metamorphosis, so we drew plenty of heat from them. Inevitably, some of my people threw their hands in the air in frustration, saying, "I don't know how we can do it. It's just not happening. It'll never happen."

At those times, I tried to be the counselor and coach, returning them to the overall game plan that we all believed would get us there. I often pointed to our performance charts, dwelling on the positive progress towards the goal, instead of the gap that still remained for us to overcome.

Depressing times cried for positive reinforcement and refocusing on the possibilities. It was usually my role to bring everyone back to the vision, seeking to reaffirm their agreement in its merit as a worthy target. Then as we walked down through the goals and objectives, I would gravitate towards our measurements. One wall of our meeting room was covered in charts that tracked our performance to our quantified objectives. Any progress at all was worthy of notation. "Hey, look at the charts. The dial is moving and if we just stay the course, the plan will work," I pleaded. I pointed out any improvement that incrementally helped our cause. In some cases, we even celebrated. "Keep your eyes on the prize and keep moving forward," I asked of them.

I made sure to highlight all improvements so that we could maintain a positive view of our execution of the game plan. To keep us grounded, however, every positive statement would be punctuated with, "There's still some room for improvement. Look at where the target is." Over that year, we constantly made the association between the performance gap and our overall plan. It was ongoing reinforcement. The team needed to see that they were improving, that there was reason for them to still believe that they could do it, while maintaining a focus on the goals.

And with that focus, an understanding of how to work the plan, and a team commitment to win, it all became a unified effort. When they made significant achievements, they didn't rest. When they eliminated the number one quality problem, the group immediately moved on to number two with the same vigor that killed the first one. The focus had become so well-tuned that the people themselves were simply intent on achieving their goals. It became a somewhat methodical and automatic approach. Over that year, we became a team that was absolutely, positively going to get where it wanted to go. They knew to execute the plan as we had discussed. The group knew to refer back to the measurements in order to check the results of their actions. And they comprehended the fact that every incremental gain must be followed by another. While it took us five more months than our original target date, we finally achieved what they had all thought was impossible. What had been created along the way, however, was a team that knew what it takes to excel.

CHAPTER 3

Use Any Unique Attribute You Have

Do not let what you cannot do interfere with what you can do.

— John Wooden
FORMER UCLA BASKETBALL COACH

THE COACH'S LESSON

The Detroit Rockies had a unique advantage in that they were an all-black hockey team. Most kids that we played against had never seen anything like us, so they didn't know what to expect. It was impossible for us to be anything but an underdog in any game we ever played. We were expected to lose since, in many people's minds, we were out of place in the sport to begin with.

The assistant coaches (fathers of two of the boys) and I would talk about this with the team. We would frame the lack of respect as an example of the world outside. Not a week went by where I didn't hear one of us saying, "No one is going to give you anything for free, including respect. You have to go out there and earn it." The boys always went into a game looking to prove someone wrong. They knew what people were thinking. They noticed people staring at the "basketball players who played hockey." That became their rallying cry.

Naturally looking for any edge, we capitalized on the fact that we had a unique attribute that could preoccupy an opponent. Our players accepted that there were some players who would hate to lose to us. They knew that other opponents who had never encountered us would be awestruck for some period of time. So we would concentrate on the first five minutes of the game differently than the rest. During the beginning moments of the game, we would try an all-out blitzkrieg of the opponent, trying to catch them off-guard.

With this twist, I modified our game plan for the first minutes of the game. We would dump the puck straight into the opposing team's end, softly enough so that the puck would come to rest against the backboards. Two of our forwards would then skate as fast as they could at the defenseman who was retrieving the puck and try to physically force a turnover. Yes, it was somewhat punishing. To borrow a line from the movie *Bull Durham*, we thought it announced our presence "with authority." The goal of this strategy was to immediately affect the opponents and have them looking over their shoulders for the rest of the game. Knowing and accepting our unique difference helped our players believe that this element of the game plan would actually work. And for a coach, anything that can inspire players' confidence in the game plan is worth every cent.

In our final tournament in Lake Placid, New York, the guys, having come to grips with this advantage, saw it as a strength and wanted to use it. Since we were playing teams from all over North America, we assumed correctly that they had never seen an all-black team. Hell, most hadn't seen a black hockey player at all! Before a key game, the captains of our team asked if they could do something different before the game started. They explained to me what they planned to do, and I agreed with a good laugh.

They asked me and the two assistant coaches to leave the dressing room before the game and go to the bench. While on the bench, we watched the opposing team step onto the ice and skate around their end zone, warming up. Our boys remained in our dressing room. They were making everyone wait. In the stands, there were hundreds of spectators, including locals who came to see the "black team from Detroit." Eventually, the referee came to the bench. "The captains have them in the room," I told him. Impatiently, the ref turned and walked towards our locker room to get the guys. And everyone waited, watching for someone to come out of the tunnel that extended from our room to the ice. Suddenly, with all the subtlety of a tornado, the boys charged out of the dressing room onto the ice, screaming as loud as they could, banging their sticks on the boards. All eyes and mouths opened simultaneously. The opposing players, having stopped in their tracks, stared. The boys then skated around in their end and, as the startled opponents watched, they returned the stares, hollering "What are you looking at?" If you can visualize this entrance, then you also can imagine how the momentum swung in our direction *before* the game even started.

Capitalize on Your Strengths

Like individual players, no two teams are alike. While it seems obvious, it's surprising that many teams fail to capitalize on their uniqueness. Too often, teams struggle to play the exact same style. Yet, each team possesses some attribute that no other team has. It might be tangible, such as a star running back, faster players that can steal more bases on a baseball diamond, or a deeper bench that can keep players fresh. Regardless, the key is to identify this attribute and use it to your advantage.

A tangible advantage is usually enough to warrant changing the game plan. Take the star running back, for example. A football coach will no doubt try to build a plan that capitalizes on the strength of this player. The running plays may be modified, or new ones created to allow this player to excel. The capability of the offensive line to execute run blocking will come under more scrutiny. The percentage of running plays versus passing plays called during a game will no doubt be skewed towards this advantage. In many ways, the game plan will be altered to make use of the team's strength.

While the unique advantage is usually tangible, it may also be intangible. It may be something that can't be quantified, such as the impact of hoards of screaming hometown fans. A home team may have the advantage of thousands of cheering fans surrounding them. Look at what some European soccer teams do to encourage that. Some have written team songs. Others have handed out colored banners or signs. They give away common colored shirts so that the fans are unified in appearance. All of this, plus some good strong stout, makes for a wild crowd, some deafening noise, and a definite home field advantage.

Your advantage can be on a purely emotional level as well. It is common for teams to react to a future opponent's negative comments to the press. How often do we hear of players clipping out newspaper articles that quote opponents' disrespectful remarks? One of the most common sources of motivation for a coach to draw upon is the underdog status. It definitely can impact the motivation level of a team and, to that end, even the outcome of the game. Whether the team's unique advantage is used to augment the game plan or simply to help motivate the players, a coach must seize this opportunity.

Players and coaches should talk about their unique strengths openly. Any advantages should be common knowledge to the team members, and team discussions should always try to focus on how to exploit them. Whether these advantageous attributes are incorporated into the game plan or simply used as a source of motivation, they can add value if the team recognizes them.

It is important that the players have confidence in the game plan. If they believe it can work, then their preparation and execution will be improved based on their belief that it will eventually pay off. Enthusiasm can grow out of that kind of thinking. And enthusiasm becomes energy, eventually. That's what a coach is after.

Lesson from a Legend: Bill Walsh

 When Bill Walsh first assumed control of the San Francisco 49ers, they were a far cry from the team that most of us think of. They had lost more games than they had won over the previous years. While gathering some good draft picks along the way, a nucleus was indeed forming. But for the time being, they were losers. With a dismal record behind them, Walsh was faced with trying to get the attention of the players, while at the same time motivating them to believe in him and his game plan. He knew he needed to quickly unite the team behind their new coach. Every player had to trust him and to focus on his game plan exclusively.

In a conversation with sportscaster Charlie Jones, former 49er offensive lineman Randy Cross described a speech that Walsh gave to his players early in his first coaching year. According to Cross, Walsh said, "Some of you are pretty good ball players, and some of you figure you can go somewhere else, and some figure, hey, if I don't make it here I can get traded. Well, I've got a news flash for you. You're on the worst team in the NFL. You were 2 and 14 last year. Who wants you? If you can't play for me and if you can't fit in with my system, you're going to be getting on with the rest of your life."

With that speech, Walsh used the losing record as a source of motivation, while at the same time reinforcing that none of them could be a winner unless the team was a winning team. He immediately established the team's focus on his game plan. They united behind him and his game plan, and the rest is history. The 49ers went on to win three Super Bowls under Walsh's leadership and a fourth shortly after his retirement under the guidance of his protégé, George Seiffert.

The Coach as Manager: Exploiting Your Differences

Throughout the world of business, we are constantly faced with advertisements that extol what is special about companies. Obviously, someone somewhere thinks they have a better idea. The most obvious differential advantage that a company can have is its product or service. If a company is marketing something that is unique and delivers some benefit that the competition cannot, then it definitely has something worth exploiting. This is the basis for most advertising today. For example, we often hear advertisements extolling who is "number one in J.D. Power rankings" or which product *Consumer's Digest* or *PC Magazine* rated "the best." We learn about the virtues of having employee owners or an environmentally friendly philosophy. Regardless of what the claim is, if it can help to advance the cause and it sets you apart, exploit it.

Unfortunately, we usually only think of competitive advantages in the context of external competition: "What do we have that the other company doesn't?" For most managers, their company's unique attribute is not so obvious. It could be as subtle as the synergy among a creative team. Whatever it is that could become a source of pride, management should endeavor to communicate it to the organization's employees. It can only help.

Defining the message to advertise is one thing; determining who is part of the audience may be another. There may be an obvious target audience for overall companies to tout their advantage to. It could be direct customers via advertising, for example. However, it's not always that straightforward to a manager. A smaller work group may not have a target audience, such as direct competitors, independent reviewers, or eventual customers. But the benefits of communicating to the employees still exist. What if employees were to become excited about the company's hot new products? Or if they were to find out that they are the only all-female department in the building? Perhaps a distribution center has state-of-the-art inventory equipment? Doesn't that become a source of pride? Maybe motivation? Can organizational confidence develop as a result? And doesn't that translate into a better game plan? It will, if the manager focuses it in that direction. Employees should know what sets apart their product or service or their organization from the rest so that they will be the first to acknowledge it. They may develop a degree of pride in and ownership of this advantage, which may eventually lead to employees doing better work.

Any work group can rally around anything that sets them apart from the rest. Of course, the difference should always be turned into a positive motivator, instead of a negative one. Many companies utilize internal competitions to inspire teams. Groups that perform the same function could be pitted head-to-head, such as sales regions competing for the greatest increase in revenue for the year. This, of course, becomes a rallying point for the group, where the natural definition of the teams becomes the difference between them.

Managers should not miss opportunities to use any unique attributes to help their own employees develop confidence in their game plan. In addition to advertising and bragging about a competitive advantage to the outside world, a company should first use its competitive edge to its own advantage.

PUTTING THE LESSON IN ACTION

At a manufacturing operation I once managed, there were two shifts of production. As had historically been the case, the day shift was staffed with all of the engineers, support staffs, and most of the management group, as well as the floor supervisors. The evening shift ran the same number of operations, but had only floor supervision as management representation. Through the years, this created an inferiority complex among the second shift supervisors.

In truth, there was no difference in the groups. Our evening shift was just as talented as the day shift; we put good people on all of our shifts. To me, it made little difference. Hey, they were all my guys, I figured, "I love 'em all the same." The evening shift personnel, however, saw it differently.

These feelings of inferiority soon became a source of inspiration for the second shift supervisors. It created a challenge where one had no reason to exist. "Yeah, we're second class citizens, but we can still outproduce you guys on day shift anytime," they would jest. They continuously tried to out-perform their day shift counterparts by producing more parts with better quality. They reveled in the fact that they could do it without any "help" from higher management or engineering support. After a while, this playful competitiveness grew to affect all of the production employees on the evening shift. Soon the entire shift was celebrating their superior performance num-bers. This only inspired them more.

In an effort to "feed the animal," I created a board that highlighted the record performances of each shift in a number of categories. This unique attribute that was alive and well in my organization was significant enough to be recognized by its own measurement. Of course, this served to inspire both groups.

Obviously, as a manager, I knew what the positive results of this "friendly competition" were going to be. So I began to use it as a source of motiva-tion. Each time a shift reached a new milestone in its measurements, we celebrated. Whether I rewarded them with coffee and donuts or simply shook their hands in front of the others, success was always acknowledged. I fre-quently made mention of the "other shift" when talking to the supervisors. "Hey, maybe you guys should work a few hours on evenings, just to see what those guys are doing differently than you," I would tease them.

My only concern was that the friendly competition might, at some point, turn unfriendly. So, I would temper my comments at appropriate times. I would always refer to "us" and "we," instead of talking about individual shifts. References were always made to the overall results for the day; one group's successful run was never allowed to overshadow the poor end result of the combined shifts. Supervisors of each shift would be enlisted to deal with common problems, underscoring that "we're all in this together."

By keeping the competition somewhat playful and still maintaining the overall focus on the whole team's success, we stayed true to our game plan. In the end, it was nothing but smiles among the gang, and good results on all of the charts and graphs.

The amazing result, however, was that all of this served to move our overall game plan forward. The groups developed confidence in their abilities, believing that they were the best. Their attitudes seemed to suggest that any initiative that could become part of the game plan would be an easy challenge for their shift. When I taught new methods and assignments, they were attentive. They brought confidence to any task that they believed they could master. Of course, they had their own causes throughout this time of competition. Each shift wanted to be the best. Regardless of their true motivation, as long their methods were focused, using common methods to achieve common objectives, we would all be just fine. And we were.

CHAPTER 4

Develop Your Playing Style Based Upon Your Players

ABILITY IS WHAT YOU'RE CAPABLE OF DOING.
Motivation determines what you do. Attitude
determines how well you do it.

— LOU HOLTZ, HEAD NCAA FOOTBALL COACH

THE COACH'S LESSON

I always had a vision in my mind of the kind of team I wanted our Rockies to become. (It really was a vision of the kind of team I wanted to coach.) I had high ambitions that they could fly across the ice, flowing through complex plays as effortlessly as our opponents seemed to do. Unfortunately, my recollection of the early years was anything but the realization of that vision.

I can remember drawing out complicated plays on the chalkboard and noticing the blank stares looking back at me. My players had a hard time following all the arrows I was drawing, which showed the simultaneous movement of players and the puck. On the ice, it was even worse. They couldn't make the crisp passes that were required, nor could they execute the quick, precisely timed movements. Unfortunately, the flashy, skilled players that I wanted to coach were not what I had to coach.

I couldn't escape the fact that my players would never be the finesse "playmakers" that I had dreamed them to be. Instead, they were fast, aggressive, and reactionary. They would charge ahead at full speed through plays that required them to take their time and move precisely. Near the other team's net, they had a bad habit of shooting the puck from anywhere without first looking for teammates. Many of my attempts to create detailed attack or breakout plays failed since they were not precision players. I could not transform them into something that they weren't. As a result, the entire first year was filled with broken plays poorly executed by frustrated players. I realized, too late for that doomed first season, that I had contributed to their failure as much as they had. By trying to fit the "proverbial" square pegs into round holes, I had led them astray.

After that first year, I gradually began to develop the playing style that best fit them. I had to capitalize on our strongest attributes. The Rockies were skaters who loved to move forward at full throttle. They played aggressively, both physically and mentally. It was "in your face, smash-mouth hockey." Focusing on our speed and aggression, I centered our new plays on intense fore-checking and dump-and-chase plays that would force turnovers. It would be perfect for us, I decided. This style of play involves a team carrying the puck towards the opposition's end and first, shooting it into their defensive zone so that the puck ends up behind their net, and then secondly, chasing after it, hoping to beat the opponents to the puck. What usually results is a race to the puck, normally ending with collision as the two players converge. It is a full-frontal attack that often catches opponents by surprise or in vulnerable positions. If it is executed properly, you will gain control of the puck deep in your opponent's end with a chance to score. It is a style of play that fits a fast team that plays well physically.

As expected, the Rockies loved these plays. They couldn't wait to chase an opponent to the puck and punish him against the boards when they got there. By catching teams off-guard in their own end of the ice, we quickly began to increase our scoring chances around the net. When the puck became ours, we would fire it towards the net immediately, ready to pounce on any rebounds. The players thrived on this type of play, since it involved their two favorite aspects of the game. I loved it because it was based on the team's two strongest qualities.

Capitalize on Players' Natural Tendencies

The fact that all teams are different poses unique challenges for coaches. Players are different, both physically and mentally. Strategies are different. Coaching styles differ. Even tangibles, such as team chemistry and home field surface, come into play. All of these ultimately contribute to the need for a distinct playing style. Every coach must accept this.

The playing style is the overall approach that a team will bring to each game plan. It is the manner in which they will execute their tasks. It will encompass specific actions that together will necessitate specific behavior and techniques. In basketball, a team with tremendous speed and rebounding may play a quick, transitional, "fast break" game. A hockey team lacking speed and finesse, but wealthy in size and aggression may develop a clutch-and-grab, physical style of play. Once a team has established a style of play that matches its players, then it will settle into good form.

A perfect example of a game plan that embraced a specific playing style was that of the San Diego Chargers of the early '80s. They were a team that passed the ball, period. They played Coach Don Coryell's "West Coast Offense," which put air under the ball in every direction of the field. Older football fans could probably name the starting quarterback, wide receivers, and tight end on the Chargers team. They might be hard pressed, however, to name any running back that was on the team. That's a reflection of the style of football that the Chargers played back then because it suited their players.

The obvious point to be made here is that any attempt to "force" a playing style onto a team that is inherently unable to adapt to it will fail. The reasons don't matter. If the members of the team don't have the capability to adapt, disaster will result.

A coach must assess players and attempt to develop the playing style that best fits the team. To do this, a coach needs to consider the players' current abilities, both physical and mental, as well as their capacity to develop and learn in the future. Coaches also need to consider how the team has played in the past. This will be the frame of reference used to contrast with all that you will attempt to teach them in the future. Without the ability to handpick players, a coach will have to adapt any game plan to match up with those who will be expected to execute it.

Many coaches would prefer to throw out the old and bring in the new. This opposite approach involves acquiring specific types of players in order to define or create a new style of play. This approach, however, can rarely translate into quick success. If the coach is able to select players, then that selection will have to take into account the kind of team that the player will be joining. Original players will have to embrace the new style, as well as the new players. A core group that enlivens the new desired style must be grown large enough to be able to carry the accompanying new game plan. The amount of time for this kind of transformation of an existing group must be comprehended and respected. For this reason, it is normally quicker to match a game plan to an existing group's style.

Lesson from a Legend: Scotty Bowman

 For the 1967–68 hockey season, the NHL was to expand from its six teams to twelve teams. As the newly hired coach of the St. Louis Blues expansion team, Scotty Bowman was initially faced with the task of drafting his team's players from a list of cast-offs that were left unprotected by the Original Six powerhouses. Along with General Manager Craig Patrick, Bowman began to plan for the draft. He knew that it would be impossible to field a team that could beat the Original Six teams regularly. These six veteran teams played a wide-open style of hockey that utilized their incredible strength, speed, and shooting firepower. The caliber of players available in the draft would have a tough time handling that type of game. Instead, Bowman believed that if the Blues could simply hold their own against the Original Six teams, they could easily win games against the new expansion teams. So the entire Blues' drafting strategy was based on doing just that—building a team that could withstand the firepower from the older franchise teams.

Bowman had determined that the Blues would need to play a defensive style of hockey. Unable to play shot for shot against the Original Six, the Blues instead would build a stronghold that would minimize the scoring chances against them, while hoping to score enough goals for them to keep the games close.

He would need players who were solid defensively with enough discipline and "hockey smarts" to play a disciplined defensive game.

Throughout that draft, they selected players who had experience and poise, including two future Hall of Famers who were quickly moving past their prime. The St. Louis Blues, as a result, iced a team that was able to win a majority of games against their peers, while managing to not be embarrassed by the Original Six teams. After winning two playoff series, the Blues played in the Stanley Cup finals in their first season, losing eventually to the Montreal Canadiens. Scotty Bowman was named Coach of the Year by *The Hockey News* in his inaugural season as an NHL coach.

The Coach as Manager: Finding Your Work Group's Natural Style

As in a sports team, style is important to any organization. Whether it is a company, department, or small work team, the same assessment must occur. A manager needs to define a playing style that will marry the employees' capabilities with the demands of the objective. All employees are different, and they will gravitate to a work style that is natural to them. Some employees are thorough and pay great attention to detail. Others may rely on more reactionary skills. So you may see some groups that plod along methodically and precisely, while others dart through tasks according to what is a priority. Some work teams seem to naturally allow freethinking and creativity, while others seem bound by perceived rules that discourage entrepreneurship.

It holds true in business, as in sports, that a group of people will find it difficult to adapt to an operating style that does not come to them naturally. In the '80s, many manufacturing organizations tried to make the transition from a disciplinary, autocratic management style to the more participative and cooperative team approach. Easier said than done. Many of the managers in leadership positions had "grown up" in the factories during the '60s and '70s. During those years, it was more typical for a manager to yell directions than to calmly ask for employees' opinions.

To make the change to a more cooperative style, all levels of management had to learn to dictate less and communicate and involve more. During that evolution, high-level leaders found that some mid- to low-level managers were incapable of this change. Keep in mind that many supervisors and managers had long been rewarded for their heavy-handed, terse approach. And now they were being asked to behave in a fashion that was completely different. Was it wrong to try to force this change in styles? Not necessarily, especially if the needs of the business environment at that time left few alternatives. The mistake made by many higher level managers was underestimating how difficult it would be for some career managers to change, how long that change would take, or whether or not it was even possible.

This highlights the importance of first matching employees' capabilities with a proposed work style. Before establishing a new style, however, consideration must be given to any opportunity to train, educate, and support employees who need to transition to a new approach. People are capable of change. Albeit difficult to initiate and manage, it is possible for an organization to "rehabilitate" employees to adapt to a new environment.

Just like a sports coach, the manager doesn't always have the luxury of eliminating employees that don't fit. In today's litigious society and with low unemployment, it is becoming increasingly difficult to fire employees. Instead, companies are forced to deal with out-of-place workers by finding them different assignments. This is a little easier for a large company, since there are so many more positions that can be filled. Smaller companies don't have such flexibility. The more realistic alternative, then, is to adapt an overall plan and style that matches the employees it impacts.

PUTTING THE LESSON IN ACTION

There were many goals that challenged my work team, and they all had the urgency of a train's whistle coming at us. Our objectives all had to be met, and they would need to happen simultaneously. This predicament, of course, is not new. It just seemed ugly at the time. It was obvious to me that we would need to be much quicker at what we did. We would need to operate in a manner that would expedite our actions, while maintaining thoroughness in our preparations.

In transforming my own team at work, I began to emphasize actions that I believed would help to create the best style for us. Just as I did for my hockey team, I had to stand back and assess my players' characteristics. Our strengths were many. The level of talent in the group was terrific. They could handle tremendous amounts of work quickly. They were all ambitious and wanted personal reward and acclaim. They were all in the same relative age group with some terrific diversity, and many were friends outside of the workplace, too. When I looked at these people, I saw a lot in common. They had the spirit, the intelligence, and the brainpower to work together and develop some synergy. "Okay," I thought, "if they have the makings of a team, then a team they'll be." That would define our style!

I kept bringing them together in groups to conduct all our business. I thought, "The more time they spend together as one team, the better chances are that they'll grow into one." We created a regular meeting schedule where we would often regroup to deal with any topic. I wanted them to act, think, and achieve as a team. Attempts by them to come to me one-on-one with group issues were met with instructions to "bring it to tomorrow's meeting for the team to consider." After a while, it became the norm that we would be meeting to review each other's details.

They learned that the entire team would determine decisions and direction and that everyone had input on any matter. They saw that the team was the central force in what we were doing. They brainstormed together. They developed initiatives together. And, as a personal prerequisite for all my meetings, they laughed a lot together. Soon they began to sense the synergy that was being created as they were "firing on all eight cylinders." Since it was a group of people who worked well together, the tighter they grew, the more they were looking out for each other. Because they all felt ownership in the team's initiatives, no one was going to let a teammate fail.

Without even realizing it, we became more efficient. Our communications were greatly improved, we made fewer mistakes, and plans were critiqued well before execution. All this came about from creating a team atmosphere. With a new ability to execute our game plan quicker, we began to set aggressive goals that pushed us to limits that we thought we couldn't reach. Our timelines became much shorter and the rate of our improvements more impressive. We were moving swiftly, establishing a new pace for our own actions. Our original plans were based on a style and approach that was already obsolete. We had taught ourselves a better way to work. So, in an attempt to establish our new style as a norm, we continued to feed it with ambitious goals. In effect, we changed our game plan's objectives to match our new work habits.

CHAPTER 5

Players Want to Believe in Their Coaches

IF ANYTHING GOES BAD, I DID IT. If anything goes semi-good, we did it. If anything goes really good, then you did it. That's all it takes to get people to win football games for you.

— PAUL "BEAR" BRYANT
FORMER FOOTBALL COACH, UNIVERSITY OF ALABAMA

THE COACH'S LESSON

So I had a good game plan. So what. It would be useless if the Rockies didn't execute it, and they wouldn't execute it if they didn't believe in it. For them to ever believe in my game plan, they had to believe in me. I knew that the only way they would follow me and take my directions or lessons well would be if they had no doubts about my knowledge. It was always important to me that the players looked up to me as a coach.

Whenever I was around them, I tried to teach them. I spent a lot of time with them individually, talking about their own skills and talents. During practices, I would often pull one guy aside at a time to give him personalized instruction on how to correct some flaw or mistake. I believed that this personal attention would help to build the individual relationship I had with each of them. That, I sustained, would be the foundation of their allegiance to me and, therefore, my plan. I figured that as long as they thought they were learning something from me, they would want to listen.

Since one of my personal goals as a coach was to deepen their understanding of their positions on the ice, we spent many hours in practice talking about what we were doing. They learned why they had to move to certain positions, not just to do it. As they began to understand how the opponent would react to what we were doing, they saw opportunities. By understanding the how's and why's, they were able to see more of what was going on around them, as well as anticipate what would happen moments later. It was this thoroughness in our preparation that expanded their confidence in my game plan and in me. And that led to the growth of their own confidence.

My pre-game preparations always involved tips about the strengths and weaknesses of the other team. For example, I had a habit of watching the opposing team's goalie during the pre-game warm-up. In the final huddles before the start of the game, I would tell my guys what aspect of the goalie's play I thought was vulnerable, what would make it easy for us to score. "Shoot to this guy's glove hand," I'd offer. "He keeps it low and tucked in too close to his body." They always seemed excited to hear those tips, as if they suddenly knew some secret about the other guy that was going to help us win. What they were doing in those moments was gaining confidence from my confidence.

As they believed in me, they believed in my game plan. Throughout that first year, they gradually increased the attention they paid my lessons. Their concentration during my drills grew more intense. Amongst each other, they were beginning to reinforce my plan, speaking the same language as I was. That was the confidence I was after: "Believe in me, believe in my plan, and then believe that you can do it."

They seemed to appreciate the details and insights that I provided them into their own play as well as the opposition's. They became aware that I was always watching them, looking for ways to help them improve. Whenever I came to them with advice, they trusted it. Although they had never actually said so, I sensed that they felt I was an asset. Then one day, in their own special way, they confirmed it. The boys were joking after practice about how our team was always playing "white teams," but that "we have the only white boy that matters." Understanding these teenaged kids and the odd way that they complimented people, I knew they were giving me high praise.

Leadership Inspires Loyalty

Just as belief in a unique attribute can serve as a source of inspiration and motivation for a team, so can the coach. Players need to have confidence in their coaches. Players want to believe in their coach's preparation of them. They want to believe that they know the opposition well, and that they have a game plan that can succeed. This feeling of confidence should add to the intensity of their practice, as well as eliminate any doubts or questions they might have during their preparation. That level of confidence can only carry into a game. If only for this reason, the coach must put the effort and thought into gaining this level of trust from his team.

A coach must work at least as hard as every player on the team. If a player cannot see intensity in the coach's approach to the game, then how much inspiration can possibly be created? Players will respond to a coach's positive work ethic and drive to succeed. Keep in mind that there is no benefit to being the stoic coach, working hard behind the scenes, hidden away from the team. The players need to see their coach's hard work, or at least know about it. They need to be aware of a coach's dedication to the task of preparing them, the players, for battle. That shows the coach's obvious commitment to doing whatever it takes to win.

Players want to hear a coach talk with authority on the subject of the team. The more a coach demonstrates how well he knows his players and his team, the more credibility he has in general. This also goes for knowledge of the team's systems, the opponents, and the game overall. Aside from credibility, this puts the coach in a position to teach the players. The opportunity to learn can only draw players closer to their coach.

The coach, of course, cannot be the expert on every aspect of the game. However, the head coach must be able to tie it all together in one overall plan. In the end, that's the most important thing players want from their coach. A player needs to concentrate only on internalizing and practicing the game plan, not on deciding whether it will work.

If the players believe in their coach, then the belief and confidence in the game plan cannot be far behind. That, ultimately, is all a coach wants. It isn't about any absurdly self-centered attempt to get players to like him. It's simply about believing in the game plan. Famous coaches such as Vince Lombardi and Scotty Bowman were hated by some of their players. But many of those players admitted in interviews that they believed in their coach's knowledge, his intuition, and, therefore, his overall plan. That's what counts most for a team to perform with confidence.

Once a team embraces their game plan and their preparation, they will comprehend their roles as never before. Knowing and internalizing the team's entire plan will better synchronize the actions of the players. As players develop an understanding of their methods, systems, and individual assignments, their mental preparation will transform their physical performance. They will develop the intuition, anticipation, and concentration that may give them the advantage over their opponent. They will see opportunities that were hidden to them before.

Lesson from a Legend: Dean Smith

 During his years at the University of North Carolina, Coach Dean Smith was well-known as an avid student of the game and of his opponents. His biographies are filled with anecdotes told by former players that describe Smith predicting the other teams' plays and even predicting the scores of games. It was as if, in many of his players' minds, he simply knew what was going to happen.

Smith studied game films religiously and watched any other games that his TV set could serve up for his appetite. Smith put so much effort into studying his opponents and preparing his team to play against them, that he himself had well-founded confidence. It was this confidence that his players drank up as they became believers in him.

In 1971, Smith's Tar Heels came off of an 18-9 season and lost an All-American guard from their starting line-up. Many experts predicted that the Tar Heels would be lucky to have a winning record. Smith thought differently. Through regular reinforcement, Smith espoused to his troops that if the group played as a team and shared one common focus as a team, they would make believers out of others, too. They ended up ranked fifteenth in the nation and won the NIT tournament that year.

In an interview with former UNC player and author David

Chadwick, Bobby Jones, another former player, talked about being coached by Dean Smith. "Coach Smith somehow, some way, made us believe that if we followed his philosophy we would win. By the time I was a senior, if he'd told me to go to the corner and stay on my hands and knees until the play was over—if he said we would win by doing that—I would have done it. We knew putting the team above the individual worked. We knew that was his vision. And we did whatever he told us because we believed in him."

Confidence in the Boss Creates Trust

In the workplace, the manager has the same need: employees must believe in the organization's plan. Like a coach, the manager needs employees to believe in him or her. Likewise, the manager has the same ability to impress and inspire. Employees can sense intensity and drive from a manager, and they will respond to it. Some employees will increase their own efforts, trying to match that of the manager. Others may falter, exposed by their apathy or incapability. Regardless, good managers must still reveal that they are fully prepared for the "game" and that they intend to win.

To successfully lead a group, a manager must be confident and knowledgeable about the team, its goals, and its potential. This not only shows employees that the manager understands the challenges they face in the pursuit of their goals, but also that he or she is confident in the group's ability to meet those challenges. Being knowledgeable may require the manager to research, study, and prepare in order to approach the work team confidently. Employees often need guidance or additional direction, and the supervising manager is usually the source. In this case, the manager's knowledge and confidence is essential to the team's success because it is also a source of confidence for the team.

This doesn't necessarily mean that the manager must be the subject matter expert. It is almost impossible for any one person to possess more knowledge than each of his or her individual "experts." However, by constantly providing informed focus, vision, and optimism, the manager will help everyone adhere to the strategy, even during hectic times.

If the manager's preparation and development of the team has been sound, then their understanding of the game plan will be sound as well. With a deep comprehension of the team's assignments and roles, the employees can move quickly, reacting accordingly to any new scenario. They will see opportunities and anticipate reactions and responses of their opponents. A higher level of personal and team performance is usually noticeable to people. As a result, the coach's thorough preparation and development of the team will become a source of motivation for them.

PUTTING THE LESSON IN ACTION

At work, I was never out to prove that I knew more than my subordinates did. I only wanted them to see me working hard to prepare them and myself for our pursuits. I never hid my intensity or my desire to win. I didn't hide my excitement over reaching milestones, nor my disappointment in setbacks. I worked long hours, not for show, but to contribute as much to the team as I wanted to see them contributing. Personally, I never wanted anyone to question my absolute desire to reach our objectives, and I was willing to sacrifice my leisure time to pursue our goal. I was always focused on my own work.

However, as I began approaching my work team more like a coach than a traditional manager, I realized I needed this team to believe in me just like my players did. I would never get them to "sign up" for my plan if they didn't think I was their guy. So began my efforts to reach my work team and expand their confidence in me.

My focus shifted more towards looking for opportunities to teach and develop my employees. Like my players, I needed them to believe in my ability to help them or to contribute to their own personal efforts. I began to spend more time gleaning information that could help them with their tasks. I looked for opportunities for them to learn. I identified obstacles and sought out support for them in order to better prepare their path. My role became one of an enabler.

Soon, I was a step ahead of them. Subordinates were pleasantly surprised when I appeared at their desks with "some information that I thought would help you." I would give out an assignment with the additional information that "I've already contacted that department head and they're preparing the information you'll need for this." During meetings, I spoke confidently of our ability to achieve, even when told of new obstacles or recent mistakes. My strong belief in our plan was unwavering, and they began to feed off of it. "This will work if we stick with it. It's working already, if you look at the charts. Learn from the mistakes and it will come," I told them.

As an enabler, I became more focused on leading them. Like a scout, I was ahead of the group, determining the best path to take, identifying what they needed to make the trip and how best to prepare them for it. As their belief in me grew, so did their confidence in my plan. They believed that I had a vision and that everything would fit together as I claimed it would. And that helped to give birth to a new team confidence that made them superior.

As their comprehension of the game plan increased, they were soon able to visualize the same results I was. They understood how initiatives would synchronize together. It became apparent to them that they could depend on simultaneous actions by their peers that would help lead to the team's success. Seeing this recognition in their eyes only inspired me to serve and motivate them more. So I reinforced them positively, encouraged them to learn from mistakes, and asked for their creative opinions. I made myself available for individual discussions, lessons, or simply to answer questions. I continued to feed this inspired group, supporting whatever needs they had.

Several employees made a point of expressing appreciation for how hard I was always working to improve the team. "You always seem to be looking out for me," one female engineer said.

"Hey," I replied, "on a team, nobody wins unless everyone wins." This personal interaction and other rewards of my new management style were much more gratifying and fulfilling than I'd ever experienced as the order-barking boss I had once been.

CHAPTER 6

If a Player Doesn't Fit With the Game Plan, Get Rid of the Player

Some of the best performers may not be the ones destined to continue to achieve...Making changes with people like these...can appear almost incomprehensible to close-knit staffs and to the outside world. But they are part of the hard task of adapting to and confronting the success syndrome.

— Bill Walsh
head coach, San Francisco 49ers

THE COACH'S LESSON

We had a rather unique situation with the Rockies. We were always desperate for players. The previous coaches and parents had tried to keep the same group of kids together throughout the years. Both the players and their families had grown close, and they all thought of the team as a second family.

That was good for us, since we didn't have the luxury of having a big team. However, that didn't mean that we would do anything to keep every player on the team. While we were starved for quality players, we actually had to release one of our guys.

This player was a talented center who had terrific speed and a great spirit. He had been with the team for several years and was good friends off the ice with many of the other players. Unfortunately, as these boys advanced through their adolescent years, they began to experience more and to be affected by their ever-expanding worlds. This kid began to hang out with the wrong crowds. Word came back to us that he was spending too much time on the streets and that we were literally losing him.

Being the family that we believed we were, some of the parents took turns trying to convince him to straighten up. He was missing practices and even some games. When he did play with us, he was always a step behind or in the wrong place. This went on for some time. It was obvious that he wasn't taking his commitment to the team seriously and that he had too many distractions in his life. Attempts to pull him back into the hockey family didn't work, and the stories that got back to us continued to get worse and worse. It was at that time that we decided to give up on him. I looked at the rest of the team and knew that they were more important.

As a coach of a group of boys in their most formative, and perhaps vulnerable, years, it was one of my desires to help develop solid, young men of whom society could be proud. It was actually part of *my* game plan, one that I shared with Alex, George, Gloria, and the other parents and guardians of the kids. We didn't just want them to win at hockey, we wanted them to win at life. We cared about the kids' grades. We kept informed about who was hanging out with whom. It was always more important for us to be positive role models to these boys. Here was a situation where it became apparent that our lost player was turning into the type of person we were trying to avoid on our team. He was becoming a distraction to our boys.

About a year after he left the team, he found his way back to the arena and showed up to watch a couple of games. It turned out that he missed hockey and was looking to skate. He had not, however, returned to school or quit the gang that he had joined. And for those reasons, we wouldn't consider allowing him back. Sure, his loss had hurt us. He was an excellent center, and we were short on that position. Hell, we were short on players, period. After a while, though, it became obvious that we were learning to play without him. The boys didn't talk about him, nor did they mention his absence in the line-up. He would have to live with the consequences of his decisions, just as the boys who decided to commit to the team were living with their decisions. To take him back would have threatened one of our overall goals for the team. So we moved on without him. The rest of the boys didn't look back.

The Team Is Always More Important Than a Single Player

Too much work goes into developing a team into a winner to let success be jeopardized by a single player. The team is always more important, and its success sacred to the coach. Anything that comes between the players and success must be dealt with, even if it is people on the team. A coach's commitment to building a winning team begins on day one and must continue steadfastly until the coach leaves. For this reason, it's not uncommon for new coaches to deal decisively with troublesome athletes in sports. How often have you seen teams make wholesale changes in personnel after a new coach comes to town?

Coaches know what type of team they are hoping to create. In developing the game plan, the coach should have already considered the skills, capabilities, and strengths of the players. So the coach then will have already tried to tailor the game plan to the players, the opponents, etc. Once the game plan is ready, the team has to move on to the development phase. At this point, if a player doesn't fit into the game plan, then he will have to be excused from it. If any player cannot, or will not, conform to the new plan, the team's progress must supersede. The bus must leave the station for the sake of the other passengers.

Casualties, at this point, are never a pleasant experience, especially if it's a veteran player. It might even be a popular player who has served the team well in the past. A soccer team trying to improve its offensive zone attack may no longer have room on the roster for an older, sure-footed defender that's been a steady player in previous years. As much as it may be upsetting to fans, a player must be let go when he no longer fits the game plan. The development of the team will suffer if the coach retains players who don't fit with the new plan.

This doesn't just apply to game-playing styles either. It could be attitude as well. Often we read about players with great dispositions who are leaders in the dressing room or teachers in practices. This is often the case with older players who have some experience and knowledge. It's their attitude that got them onto a team that is trying to become more disciplined and mature. Conversely, a player with an immature attitude that leads to confrontations with either coaches or players will probably lose his spot on the same team.

The same applies for commitment. All players must be committed to apply themselves to their assignments and to make the necessary contributions. They must be mature enough to put aside personal issues and give themselves to the group. If they are not fully and completely committed to a team effort centered around the game plan, then they become a liability.

A player that lacks the necessary skills poses a different challenge for the coach. Since it is his or her responsibility to create the support level of the game plan pyramid, the growth and nurturing of players' skills is a primary duty of the coach. If a player has the potential to develop the skills needed in a time frame that is acceptable, the coach has to take on this challenge. The coach must try to develop and train that player. However, if the player cannot grasp new concepts or master new skills over a longer period of time, the coach must accept the prospect of moving on without that player. Of course, if the player simply doesn't have what it takes to play at the team's level of competition, it is a simpler decision yet.

Lesson from a Legend: Scotty Bowman

In the late 1990s, Scotty Bowman coached the Detroit Red Wings to two Stanley Cup Championships. Earlier, during his rebuilding years in Detroit, Bowman was establishing a new game plan for the team. It involved a significantly more defensive approach to playing, punctuated with the use of a defensive neutral zone trap called the "Left Wing Lock." This was not an easy transition for the Red Wings, who had traditionally been a highly offensive team.

The team captain, Steve Yzerman, had been one of the league's top offensive players for all of his career; however, he had never won a Stanley Cup. A stoic and consistent leader of his team, Yzerman was willing to channel 110 percent of his effort in any direction, as long as that direction was towards the Stanley Cup. However, when Bowman took the reigns of the team, introducing his new game plan, Yzerman was faced with a major decision. He would have to change his entire style of play, going from a fairly one-dimensional goal scorer to a multi-dimensional, offensive/defensive player. Many players have failed at this kind of transition before. Bowman admits that there have been players throughout his career who could not adapt to his team's game plan and, as a result, were replaced. While replacing or releasing players is one of the more difficult acts for a coach, it is a necessary one. With confidence in his game plan, Bowman needed players who were dedicated to, and capable of, playing within its boundaries.

Yzerman, however, was different. "Stevie is such a competitor," Bowman says with affection. "He was willing to do anything in order to win." Throughout the tough years of adapting to Scotty's new game plan, Yzerman often talked about how much of a struggle it was for him. Ultimately he persevered. In the Red Wings' fourth year under Bowman, they ended the longest Stanley Cup drought of any team in the NHL. During their drive to the Cup, Steve Yzerman's teammates responded to his intense level of play. Many times during the crucial playoffs, Yzerman was sacrificing everything in a defensive manner, including dropping to the ice to physically block slapshots directed at his goalie.

There were players who couldn't make the transition that Yzerman did and were forced to move on. Arguably the most successful coach in the history of hockey, Scotty Bowman knew that players have to fit with the team's game plan. In the end, those that did hoisted the Stanley Cup two years in a row.

The Coach as Manager: When Employees Become Obstacles

The business world is evolving every day, and with that comes new challenges for every organization. This requires that an organization regularly tweak its game plan to fit any new requirements of the industry. Adversity is a constant. However, nothing can be allowed to get in the way of progress. It is a cold fact that includes people. If an organization has defined its direction and identified the areas where a new style or some different skill set is necessary, then it must proceed. As in the animal world, this is a completely natural and unavoidable evolution. It is the process that leads to survival or extinction.

Since the overall game plan takes the team's strengths and weaknesses into account, the necessary abilities of the employees should already be comprehended. The manager should have some predefinition of the minimum requirements from employees. Additionally, any accommodations that need to be made for employees will have been accounted for, as well. Therefore, there remains little room for compromise.

Consider a sales organization that has relied on traditional methods using salespeople making personal calls and placing customer orders through fulfillment centers. With the introduction of e-commerce, the sales industry now has a new medium to reach customers. What happens to salespeople when the company begins marketing and selling over the Internet? With customers' orders automatically triggering warehouse disbursements, what happens to clerks that no longer have orders to process? If the company now requires sales representatives and order clerks to be adept with the Internet, then that dictates a new skill set for them. As part of this process, a salesperson may be identified as one who does not possess those capabilities, and, therefore, does not fit into the plan.

Once identified as a potential problem, the employee's abilities will have to be addressed. If it's possible to develop the skills, then the manager must commit to that effort, as long as it is possible. Keep in mind, though, that timing may be critical to the game plan, so the employee's opportunity to develop his or her skills may be limited by a "deadline." The manager may simply run out of time. If the employee cannot grasp the new skill set, then he or she must be replaced.

Beyond skills, a lack of attitude or commitment to the game plan may also be reason to remove an employee from the team. It could be a clash of styles between a long-time employee and a paradigm-breaking new boss. Or think about the above example with the sales organization. If one of the veteran salespersons thought that any involvement in the Internet was a silly venture, how well will that salesperson endorse the game plan? If the salesperson spoke out against the manager's plan, how would he or she impact the focus and concentration of the other salespeople? While again allowing some amount of time for the employee's transformation, any negative influence must be corrected. If it cannot, then it must be eliminated for the good of the team.

The manager is the only person who owns this responsibility. As such, he or she must look for any clashes that might hinder the group's progress. The manager should weigh the skills and contributions of the questionable employee with the impact on the performance of the organization. If the fit does not exist and efforts to correct the situation have failed, then the person has to be removed.

This does not necessarily mean discharge. Retraining employees is an option, as well as reassigning them to another position. Every person has some strengths. Just because their strengths don't align with the needs of a particular group doesn't mean that they won't be of value elsewhere in the organization. Whatever is the best option for the overall organization will dictate the final action. The bottom line remains the same: It is up to the manager to protect the game plan and to remove obstacles for his or her subordinates.

PUTTING THE LESSON IN ACTION

Our organization went through some monumental cultural changes over a period of five years. During that time, our top management team completely upset the country club atmosphere that had existed in the facility. While performance goals were not being met throughout the previous years, the lowest levels of management were sitting back relaxing, completely oblivious to it. As a result, the entire workforce had become complacent.

We in the top leadership of the facility met to define our direction and to create our executable plans. But as we began to travel the course that we had laid out, we were met with strong resistance from some managers and supervisors. People resisted the culture change. Suddenly, the quiet, easy life that some management people had enjoyed was being violently disrupted. Our efforts received naturally hostile receptions. In fact, we found some supervisors were completely uncooperative to the point of sabotaging our efforts. As a result, we began to identify people who we did not believe were going to fit into our new organization.

Nobody enjoys this kind of phase in the development of an organization. It's ugly, it's messy, and it doesn't make you feel good. But it was a necessary phase in the evolution of our organization. Those people who needed to change were involved in efforts to facilitate it. We didn't want to be distant. We wanted to "save" as many of these detractors as possible. Others were offered detailed performance improvement plans with timelines associated for behavior changes. Eventually, the people who could not, or would not, alter their attitude or behavior were dealt with accordingly. There simply was no choice. We had to eliminate the obstacles that stood in the way of our progress.

What's not always obvious to the manager is the impact that someone's negative behavior can have on the more positive employees. In many cases, I underestimated how much the "good" people were noticing, and grumbling about, the "bad" people. In fact, many of these "good" employees stepped forward and positively reinforced our actions, commenting on how much of a distraction these people had been.

Of course, the other message this type of extreme action communicates is a dedication to the plan. It really showed how far we were willing to go. Our actions underscored our dedication to the overall plan that we were championing. Since we had a game plan in place and the support of a tremendous number of people who stood ready to act, we had to remove the people who were only going to interfere with our efforts. In the end, the progress was well-defined and quick and the remaining group of people was a stronger team for it.

The Game Plan Pyramid—Vision through Specific Actions

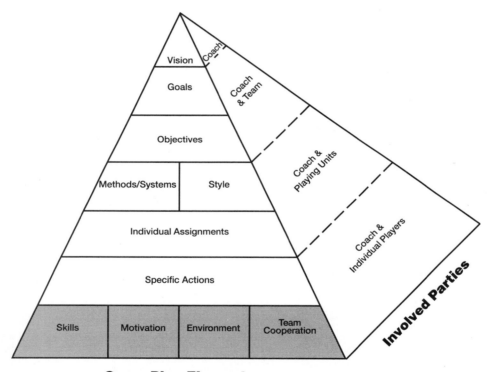

Game Plan Elements

How You Can Create a Winning Game Plan

GOALS

➤ **Step 1: Set your department's goals.**

Use the *vision* communicated from higher management to develop your department's goals. Whether higher management has dictated your department's goals to you or you are developing them, make sure they are:

___ **Ambitious, yet attainable**—The goals should force the group to reach beyond what they normally achieve, but must also be within their reach. Goals must also have a chance to succeed: Your team must not only be capable of achieving the goals, but you must be in a position to support your team in achieving them.

___ **Customer driven**—The goals must not only meet the needs and requirements of your customers, but they also must impact your customers positively or the effort will be wasted.

___ **Competitor focused**—Assess the performance of the competition, especially those factors leading to your competitors' success. By establishing your department's goals, you should be challenging your competition to a race for customers and market share.

___ **Relevant to your organization's vision**—The goals must be in direct support of the overall vision or your efforts won't help your organization become or achieve what it desires.

___ **In line with your organization's values**—Achieving your goals should never compromise the values of your organization.

➤ **Step 2: Share the goals with your team.**

For the goals you have identified, use the following checklist to share the goals with your team. Don't assume team members will know what to do without specific direction tied to goals.

❑ Paint a picture of how achieving the goal will not only help the organization but also the team and the individual players. To do this, consider:

___ Leading your team in a visioning exercise. If the goal were being achieved, how would the team be operating? What kinds of things would be happening? What would the situation look like?

❏ Give team members a chance to react. The goal may seem impossible to them at first. Allow them to express these feelings. After all, if they never accept the goal, they'll never accomplish it. If team members have trouble accepting the goals, try this approach:

___ Create an open dialogue with the team to explore all of the obstacles they believe might prevent the achievement of the goal.

___ Help the team see these obstacles as challenges to be overcome.

___ Brainstorm on ways to overcome each obstacle by working with the team to identify their unique attributes—the specific characteristics that will help them accomplish the department's goals.

OBJECTIVES

➤ **Step 1: Work with your team to set objectives.**
For each goal you identified, work with your team to set objectives that are specific, measurable accomplishments that must be achieved in order to reach the goal. Consider such factors as:

❏ Time frame

❏ How much you need to increase or decrease specific productivity, sales, quality levels, etc.

❏ Numerical targets you need to hit

➤ **Step 2: For each objective you identify, perform a *gap analysis*.**
A gap analysis will help you establish the specific actions you and your team need to take to achieve each objective. To do this:

❏ Identify the specific objectives that your team is accomplishing today.

❏ Identify the specific objectives that your team needs to accomplish.

❏ Identify the differences between what your team is accomplishing today and what they need to accomplish to reach the stated objectives.

❏ Identify all of the obstacles that could prevent your team from achieving the stated objectives.

METHODS/SYSTEMS & PLAYING STYLE

➤ **Step 1: Brainstorm on new methods and systems that will overcome each obstacle.**
For each obstacle that is within your ability to control, identify the best solution to eliminate the obstacle. To help with this brainstorming session:

❏ Consider the methods and systems being used by other organizations.

❏ Review the methods and systems previously used by your department or organization.

❏ Ask yourself and your team: If all of these methods and systems were in place, would we be likely to achieve our goals?

➤ Step 2: Define your team's playing style.

As you work through this exercise, gauge the team's manner and mindset, as well as their group and individual strengths and weaknesses. This will help you identify the team's *playing style*, which will be important when you reach Step 3.

❏ Identify your team's current playing style.

❏ Identify the type of playing style you'll need to meet your goals. To do this, build on your team's strengths.

❏ Communicate the desired playing style to your team. Be explicit and clear about your expectations.

❏ Reinforce the new playing style whenever possible.

➤ Step 3: Select the new method(s) and system(s).

Select the combination of method(s)/system(s) that best match your team's playing style and are the most feasible to implement.

PLAYING STYLE

❏ Compare each new method and system to your team's playing style.

❏ If a method won't work because of team style, first try to find a method that better fits your team's playing style.

❏ If you can't find a method/system that matches your team's playing style, you may have to take action to change the style. This is a drastic step; be sure it's worth it!

FEASIBILITY

Consider such factors as:

❏ Manpower

❏ Time

❏ Budget

❏ Other necessary resources

INDIVIDUAL ASSIGNMENTS

➤ **Step 1: Map out the *process flow*.**
For each method/system, identify the sequence of steps/actions needed to implement it.

❏ Note the critical steps, sequences, deadlines, and communication that will need to occur.

❏ Identify what the decision points are and when they should come into play. Be sure to describe the resulting actions as well.

❏ Include checkpoints to ensure that the method/system is being implemented correctly.

➤ **Step 2: Create the individual assignments.**
Based upon your analysis of the process flow, develop specific executable assignments for each individual on your team. To do this:

❏ Identify each work unit and/or individual to be involved.

❏ Assign responsibility for each executable.

SPECIFIC ACTIONS

➤ **Step 1: Define individual executable actions.**
Create job instructions for groups and individuals that are based on the assignments you made. Don't forget to:

❏ Break all assignments down into actions that can be taught, practiced, executed, and evaluated.

❏ Document all required actions.

➤ **Step 2: Define your expectations.**
By documenting your expectations for each action, you will find it easier to review with employees on a regular basis. The documented job instructions and expectations can also serve as the basis for future performance reviews.

❏ For each required action, specify your expectations with regard to:

___ Timing requirements

___ Responsibility and accountability

___ Decisions to be made

___ Standardized tasks

___ Guidelines for conduct

___ Quality of work

The Business of Winning

Section 2

Develop the Players and Their Roles

*WE STRESS THE POINT frequently that coaching
is teaching of the highest degree,
and a good coach is a good teacher.*

— PAUL "BEAR" BRYANT
FORMER FOOTBALL COACH, UNIVERSITY OF ALABAMA

A lot has to come together for a team to win: players, coaches, a good game plan, adequate reaction to opponents. True, a lot rides on the coach's shoulders; he has to prepare an overall strategy and a detailed plan to win. However, the best-coached football team will still lose if its players miss tackles or abandon their positions. Regardless of how good a game plan is, it's worth nothing if it is not executed properly. *The players have to play.* More specifically, the players have to play their positions—and their roles. So, with an adequate game plan in hand, the focus must now turn towards the teaching, training, and motivation of people.

A coach's single greatest task is the development of his players. Think of your vision of an improving team. What will it take to transform a losing team into a winner? Players have to improve their skills. Skills need to be nurtured and developed. Players need to increase their understanding of their roles. The team's game plan must be internalized. The correct moves must become reflexive, not forced. They have to play together as if they share the same mind. Obviously, then, it's the coach's ability as a teacher that truly separates excellent coaches from mediocre ones.

Like the sports coach, the role of teacher is critical to the success of any business manager. It's an aspect of the job that too often gets shortchanged in time and priority. However, the employee's need to develop never disappears, nor does the manager's responsibility to provide development opportunities. These learning opportunities are imperative to the success of the organization.

Now let's be straight about one thing: we are not talking about the traditional "education and training" of employees here. Sending people off to classes or seminars to learn new skills certainly can add value. However, it's only effective if it is performance based and relevant to the employee's position. Furthermore, such training is only a small part of what a true learning and growing organization needs. For example, sitting through a lecture on how to use a new e-mail system may be pretty boring. A hands-on training class might be more useful. But a session on specific ways to use the new system to improve communications within a department is even better.

What our organizations need involves so much more. We need to create autonomy in work groups that is guided by an overall understanding of the team's purpose. We need employees to be able to make decisions, to act and react within boundaries that are laid out in the best interests of the whole team. Business teams need independent thinkers who can focus on group activities. Businesses need *team players!* As managers, we must take individual employees and mold them into team members. Each individual must share the same understanding of the overall purpose, style, and objectives of the organization. Our employees need to understand what they are supposed to do, why they need to do it, and who or what they will impact if they do it poorly. We need the team members to mesh with the team's game plan, and vice versa.

Understandably, this is not a common line of thinking when talking about developing employees. It isn't normal for us to think this deeply about forming a team. Usually, the chaos that is part of our businesses doesn't allow us the time to do so. And unfortunately, not everyone may be good at teaching and guiding people. However, this is a line of thinking and performance that we as managers have to engage in to be successful. We owe it to our organizations, our customers, and our team members.

This approach demands that managers take a step back from the details of the daily activities and begin to look at the work group as a team. This necessitates paying attention to what your people are doing and how they are working, not just looking at the results. It requires observations on how they are interacting with each other, not assumptions that if there are no fights in the hallway, they're getting along just fine. There are more measures that indicate how well a team is functioning than just the bottom line or, in sports analogy, the win-loss column.

Establishing roles for players and groups is a critical part of a team's development, and it is a task that cannot be short-changed. It should also follow a clear path of evolution. Any team's attempt to master an overall plan must be based on a foundation of the right behavior. That's why it is important for any team to **master the basics.** Once a group has established a baseline of skills and knowledge, it can then become focused on the challenges or competition. With a well-structured game plan in hand, a coach should then look to **prepare the team to play against the opponent.** This preparation is difficult, time-consuming, and will require countless hours of work by all members of the team and coaching staff. For this reason alone, **practice is as important as the game** to any team. As the team becomes comfortable with the game plan and begins to practice executing it, each individual will settle into his or her assignment. To put a well-balanced and complete team on the playing field, **every player must have a role.** Since these roles may differ significantly, the development of individuals and groups may also take various forms. A coach must understand how and why there are differences and must be prepared to **coach the team, coach the unit, and coach the player.**

CHAPTER 7

Master the Basics

---

*DO THE ORDINARY THINGS, in an
extraordinary way.*

— GEORGE ALLEN
FORMER NFL COACH,
LOS ANGELES RAMS, WASHINGTON REDSKINS

THE COACH'S LESSON

While I was teaching the Rockies how to play their positions, we were losing a lot of games. The teams that were beating us had already moved beyond learning their positions and were executing simple plays and using various formations. It was gut-wrenchingly painful to watch. Hating to lose, I would walk away from the bench overwrought with frustration and disappointment. I told myself I had to get used to it, that it was all for a purpose. I had to learn to accept these losses.

Now, recognize that to "accept losing" is not as easy as it sounds. Patience is at a premium during these periods. It is all too easy to ignore the learning curve and try to circumvent it. But the learning curve has to be respected. If you're trying to teach someone a skill that is unusual to him or her, the time to adapt may be lengthy. Coaching, at these times, can be trying. People learn at different speeds and in different ways; this can't be helped. The learning curve may be easier for some to scale than others, but it exists for everyone. So I had to resolve myself to the fact that our hockey team would lose more than we would win if I continued to spend time building the foundation.

Soon after taking over the Detroit Rockies, I came to grips with my biggest problem: The boys had developed skills and talents, but they had never truly learned a total team game. Their style of play was individualistic and selfish. As a result, it was also disorganized. This meant that I would have to spend time teaching them the basic aspects of how to play their positions and how to play them all together as a team. Not an insurmountable task, but a formidable one nonetheless. And so it began.

I spent a great deal of the first year teaching the same things over and over. We practiced formations and positional play in slow motion without a puck. I made them stand on spots on the ice while I explained the importance of that position during a game. I worked on their skating skills, their passing methods, and their on-ice posture—all things that they should have known already from years of playing hockey. We spent over an hour a week just shooting the puck at the goalies while I instructed one player at a time. Then, the next week, I taught it all over again. The boys would roll their eyes when I explained the agenda for that night's practice and groan, "Not again!" They would plead with me that they had indeed learned the lessons and "can we please just scrimmage now?" But the lessons didn't stop. In fact, the lessons continued until I was convinced that it was second nature to them. Even then, at the first sign of a relapse in a game, we would be lining up for the same drills at practice next week.

During this period, we lost a lot of games. However, it couldn't be avoided. To play at the higher level that we were moving towards, we had to elevate our playing style. To that end, it was mandatory for us to have a solid foundation built on the basics. That was a learning curve that couldn't be shortened. It had to be respected. The cost of that learning curve was a long losing season. The benefit was tremendous success in the future.

There Are No Shortcuts to Basic Skills

The basics in team sports are easy to identify. Dribbling, passing, and shooting in basketball. Passing, blocking, and tackling in football. Pitching, hitting, and fielding in baseball. No game plan could ever be created that can overcome the absence of these basic player skills. However, as many coaches know, it may be necessary to teach a player a basic skill that probably should have been learned a long time ago. Complex plays won't work if even one player is unfamiliar with fundamental plays; therefore, a good coach teaches the basics whenever necessary.

In spite of the potential to slow the team's development process, spending time on basic skills cannot be circumvented. There may be instances where players may be lacking in some fundamental skills or knowledge. These instances might require first-time lessons for players. Concepts or movements that are foreign to some players may be tougher to learn initially. The time to teach these basic lessons may delay some of the more ambitious goals of the coach. However, if it's needed, a coach must be committed to teaching the basics, and to the time that it will take. It will only help to create a better foundation for more complex lessons later.

Often we hear professional coaches talk about "rebuilding years" or announce that they have a "three-year plan." This refers to more than just drafting and signing better players. This shows a coach who recognizes that it will take some time to lay the groundwork. The coach may want the players to change their whole style of play, or their approach to certain situations. Remember the layout of the game plan pyramid: the methods and systems will dictate the assignments, which then will dictate the techniques and behavior. It will take time for a team to learn to play a certain style. It'll require hour after hour of the same lessons, until the foundation is solid. In many cases, players may need to learn a different format or style. They may have to change the way they've played for years. In the early phase of a team's development, that is exactly why the basics have to be reinforced regularly. In these instances, patience is a virtue for both players and coaches. Players may get tired of hearing the same message over and over. This is especially true when they're losing and looking for the coach to produce some magical elixir. Even then, you must continue to take opportunities to reinforce the basic lessons. Unfortunately, there is no substitution for repetition in teaching.

Lesson from a Legend: John Wooden

 During his tenure at UCLA, Coach John Wooden was known for his absolute dedication to the preparation of the team. Everything he did had a purpose. He believed in attention to details. In fact, he strove for the perfection of those details. Players might have been surprised at some of the petty issues that Coach Wooden turned into a big deal, but there was always a reason.

The first thing players learned every season was how to put on their socks. This had to be done according to a precise method, outlined for the players, that involved several steps in actually putting the socks on, followed by a careful inspection for any creases. But when you listen to Wooden tell it, it makes all the sense in the world. In his book, Wooden explains, "This may seem like a nuisance, trivial, but I had a very practical reason for being meticulous about this. Wrinkles, folds, and creases can cause blisters. Blisters interfere with performance during practice and games. Since there was a way to reduce blisters, something the player and I could control, it was our responsibility to do it."

In another exercise, Wooden focused on the correct way to tie a shoe so laces don't come undone in a game. He also implemented strict rules on hair length because long hair can get in a player's eyes, and on drying hair after practices to reduce the chances of catching a cold. By stressing these issues, Wooden was teaching his players to control any element they could. He also ingrained in them a strong sense of discipline and the attention to detail that they would need to be champions.

The Coach as Manager: Developing Employees

In the workplace, we find ourselves doing just the opposite sometimes: not spending enough time teaching the basics. Too often, pressures from shareholders or higher management emphasize the need for immediate results. This often forces managers into becoming involved on a lower level, mired in fine details, rather than focusing on the long term. This can lead to micromanagement, poor forward planning, and a lack of an overall vision.

Instead of creating an organization that could win on its own in the future, managers only add to the daily mayhem and chaos.

Like the coach, the manager's most important role is in the development of his employees. It is up to the manager to build the foundation of solid skills and knowledge, supplementing it with the necessary support influences. He or she must create a learning environment where the development and growth of both the individual and the team is imperative. Here the manager must focus on the bottom level of the pyramid and build a foundation of excellence based on the basics.

The manager must know what the basics are and look for their evidence in employees. What are the basics in business? They are the executables that must exist in order for a company to survive, the ones that are essential to the work group's ability to deliver high-quality goods or services to their customers. For an accountant, it might be a knowledge of tax laws. At a water treatment facility, it might be the adherence to quality control checks. In a hotel, it could be the adherence to defined cleaning methods for house-keeping staff.

It's unrealistic to think that an organization can achieve any sustainable positive results if its employees are not disciplined and regimented when it comes to performing the basics. Imagine, for example, a data analysis center where employees working with computer programs are interpreting scores from customer surveys. Would the efficiency and effectiveness of the operation be impacted if some of the employees were less than proficient with the computer program? Or if some of the employees were weak in their understanding of statistical analysis? Of course, they would. But these tasks are not part of any new initiative. On the contrary, they are the basics.

It would be a mistake for a new manager to assume or take for granted that a solid foundation of common practices exists anywhere. Years of service do not guarantee proficiency in the basics. It is better to recognize any deficiencies up-front, lest future initiatives be ruined as a result.

PUTTING THE LESSON IN ACTION

A number of years ago, before I began applying my coaching methods in the workplace, I remember trying to manage chaos. Every day seemed to be a struggle. We were building a brand new product, and we were trying to do it with new equipment. We just couldn't seem to master either of them very quickly. To make matters worse, we had a workforce that had been undisciplined in their work habits and we lacked any formal structure to our actions. Not a good scenario for a manufacturing operation.

At the same time, the entire corporation was getting organized to implement common methods and procedures in an effort to create one universal manufacturing system. We were excited to learn about the new system. It was world class. It was just what we wanted our company to look like. It was sheer genius. The only problem was that we couldn't handle it.

But oh, how we tried. We attempted to implement new procedures and to institutionalize new processes. We scrambled to standardize every new strategy and initiative that cascaded down to those of us at the plant level. We met with employees to explain and teach. We personally got involved in defining the details. And yet, every time some of us turned our backs to the action, the new systems failed. Unfortunately, we simply weren't good enough to handle them yet.

The fact is, we couldn't get a break in the action to start and finish any of them. I was constantly frustrated that we could never seem to gain any stability in our operations in order for the new systems to become institutionalized. It was like that classic *I Love Lucy* episode with Lucy standing at the candy shop assembly line—we had our hands full while more was coming at us.

That's when the coach stepped in. Thinking back to my approach at the hockey arena, I recognized the root of the problem was that we, as an organization, lacked discipline. We were not performing the basics well, or regularly. No wonder we couldn't sustain any of the more complicated stuff! Too many of our employees were not good at executing the basics. We were implementing new quality control procedures, trying to meet international quality standards, yet we had machine operators who never inspected the parts they produced. All of our intentions to learn and grow couldn't save us from ourselves.

Wow. Our approach had to change. We had to become good at the basics. No, beyond that, the basics had to become completely reflexive to us. We had to become great at the basics. It had to be so abnormal for us to fail to execute a basic requirement that it would stand out and be corrected immediately. That's how good we had to be. That's what we had to do.

Realizing the solution was the easy part. Making it happen was difficult. Add making the results actually last when we turned our backs—now that was really tough! It took constant reinforcement, a lot of commitment, and a good amount of discipline by us managers.

We first had to identify what the basics were. Once we had identified the fundamental actions—the "absolutely must do wells" of our activity—we documented them like crazy. We created standardized instructions for everything associated with these actions. Regardless of how simple the instruction seemed, we wrote it down. There would be no room for guessing. We taught these instructions to everyone involved and posted them in the immediate area. And then we audited. And audited again. We verified that operators were following their instructions to the letter. We rechecked parts and compared them to the scores from the inspector. If it was supposed to be done, then someone else was going to verify it and the results would be posted visually so that anyone could verify as well. It took daily practice and regular routines by low level employees. It took regular attention from managers. It was audits and checklists and standardized work elements.

By developing a strong attention to detail and a disciplined approach, we became ready to implement more complex methods and systems. We performed the basics well, and we did it with the level of discipline and intensity that prepared us for more. We took on the company's new program, and we implemented faster than we thought we ever could have. Eventually, we became one of the model plants for the new manufacturing system in the entire corporation.

CHAPTER 8

Prepare the Team to Play Against the Opponent

IF THE COMPETITION HAS LAPTOP COMPUTERS and you're still using yellow legal pads, it won't matter how long and hard you work, they're going to pass you by.

— BILL PARCELLS, FORMER NFL COACH, NEW YORK JETS, NEW ENGLAND PATRIOTS, NEW YORK GIANTS

THE COACH'S LESSON

Developing a sports team cannot be done in a vacuum. The outside world, in this case, the opposing competition, must be taken into account. The measuring stick is obvious in sports. If you can't beat another team in head-to-head competition, then you lose. Therefore, a coach must take the competition into account when creating all elements of the game plan.

While standing behind the bench during hockey games, I would take detailed notes about our competition. I would do the same immediately after the games. Knowing that the Rockies would eventually play those teams again later in the season, I wanted to be ready for them. In tournaments, I would watch as many of the other teams play as possible—before we ever met them on the ice. The players caught on to this habit of mine after a while. They knew that I would always have hints or tips about the opposing team. They expected to have the plays tweaked here and there for a particular team. At tournaments, several of them would actually accompany me to scout our future opponents. We were always looking for some aspect of the other team's game that we could exploit.

I incorporated these aspects into our game plan and into our pre-game preparations. As a coach, I tried to utilize the same technique that the pros used and set up simulated drills during practice sessions. These mock situations pitted a group of first-string players against a group of teammates who would play and react as the opposition might. Since I'd studied the opposing teams, we could predict how they might set up and how they would attack us. So we practiced against that.

In the playoffs, where we would play a single team in an extended game series, we would often simulate game situations. Knowing that the other team played a certain formation in their own end, we would set up one of our lines to play that way in practice. We could then better develop the plays we would use in games and give the players experience playing against it.

On our team, one particular threesome always played together because their playing styles had a lot in common. My "checking line" was comprised of three fairly intelligent players who understood the game well, but weren't necessarily my top players. They were used primarily as a defensive unit to play against the opposition's best offensive line. I schooled my checking line on the formations or plays that the opponent normally used. In practice drills, their job was to act as the opposition. They would set up and play according to the guidelines that we discussed beforehand, and they would proceed to challenge the other lines accordingly. This obviously was a tremendous learning opportunity for the players who were lined up against the checking line, since it simulated a game-time situation. The other benefit was this: since the checking line would be working against the other team's top line, this exercise gave them a different perspective and understanding of how the opponent would play, thus making this defensive threesome a little smarter offensively.

Study the Competition and Modify the Game Plan

Establishing a good foundation in the necessary behavior and skills is just the beginning of the lessons. Eventually, the scope of instructions has to grow beyond the individual development of players and begin to encompass the challenges of an opposing team. To identify those challenges, as previously explored, the coach's development of the game plan becomes a prerequisite for the next stage of the team's development.

We must realize that the game plan is dynamic. It may be modified as needs arise or as opponents change. Since it is a blueprint to winning, it has to take into account the challenges that will be faced. If it is not tailored in some form to best an opponent, then what good will it be? Losing is not validation of a game plan. Only winning is. For that reason alone, it is up to the coach to know the opponent and to adapt the game plan to match up best with that opponent.

If a coach has done his or her homework, the opposition will have been analyzed and modifications made to the team's game plan. However, while the other team's strengths and weaknesses must be taken into consideration, they cannot be reason to turn the team's game plan upside down. When a game plan is being developed, a coach should always refrain from straying too far from the team's normal playing style. Many teams fall into the trap of trying to match an opponent's playing style when it is drastically different from their own. If a hockey team is normally all speed and finesse, then it will have a difficult time trying to adopt a bump-and-grind, physical style of play. Rarely does a team exist that can easily transition from one style to another and still win consistently.

Turn the Game Plan into an Action Plan for Players

As it is in the definition of the game plan, knowing the opponent intimately is necessary in the team's preparation as well. A coaching staff should have studied the opposition, made comparison notes, and identified potential mismatches prior to preparing the team. Reviewing game films and advanced scouting are regular activities of any good coaching staff. It is primarily up to the coaches to educate their team about the strengths and weaknesses of the opponent. Coaches should never assume that players remember their last game against that particular team.

A good game plan builds on the team's strengths and minimizes the impact of the weaknesses. By identifying these strengths and weaknesses, and adapting an overall game plan to them, the chances for success will increase. A coach who knows that an opposing defensive line is strong against the run on the left side obviously needs to think twice about where the team should run the ball. The challenge for the coach is to identify these mismatches before the game and compensate for them as much as possible.

The coach's focus then turns towards preparing the team. Emphasizing the coach's role as teacher, the task now becomes transferring that intimate knowledge of the opposition to the players. To achieve this goal, regular pre-game activities should include team meetings to review films, discuss game plans, identify hypothetical situations, and reexamine players' individual roles. In these forums, dialogue between coaches and players can enhance the game plan and eliminate oversights.

After the coach has communicated the game plan and observations regarding the opposition, the loop must be closed. Individual and team assignments must be modified or created to counter what has been learned about the opponent. This is the point where the game plan becomes the action plan for individuals. Deliverables are outlined, specific instructions defined, and personal roles emphasized. It's these elements that need to be communicated to players in order to bring closure to the game plan's accommodations for the next opponent. Every player needs to internalize the game plan's modifications so that, at game time, they each have specific tasks in mind that they need to execute.

For example, a basketball coach may find it necessary to modify the team's game plan to match up against a taller, stronger team that guards the basket well. This might translate into a game plan that emphasizes more movement of the ball away from the basket in order to create better shooting opportunities. New plays designed to accomplish this goal will require players to move and position themselves differently. And that is what is taught in practice.

Lesson from a Legend: Vince Lombardi

 In 1949, Vince Lombardi was an assistant coach for Army working for the legendary Red Blaik. In an age where studying game film was relatively unknown, Lombardi spent hours watching film of a future opponent, the University of Michigan Wolverines. Army would meet a Wolverine team that was seemingly invincible, having been unbeaten in two seasons and ranked number one in the nation. The coaching staff labored over the question: how could they beat this unbeatable team? Lombardi knew they needed an edge. Being one for detail, Lombardi studied films. He poured over game films from any Michigan game he could find, noting everything he could. Scribbling notes in front of the screen, Lombardi rewound play after play.

The observations that resulted did give Army the edge they were looking for. "It's surprising how many players tipped by the position of their feet, the angle of their body. You could tell whether it was a wedge play, a pass play, dive play, sweep," Lombardi remarked later in retrospect. Additionally, it was noticed that Michigan's defensive linemen were tall and, due to a high center of gravity, could easily be moved and blocked. The coaching staff eventually made "books" of their notes on opposing formations and players.

During that week's preparations, Lombardi coached his offensive linemen on how to block the taller Michigan defenders. Lombardi even went so far as to assume the stance against his players to personally demonstrate the techniques. The preparation paid off as Army went on to defeat Michigan 21-7 in that game.

The Coach as Manager: Know the Opposition

To beat any competition, you first must get to know it (or them). You can never expect to master your competition if you fail to understand why they are a viable alternative for your customers. Competitive advantage is all about one-upmanship. Being able to deliver something to the customer that the other guy can't. We need to keep in mind, however, that to exploit the competition's weakness must be within the capabilities of our own organization. All the more reason for a manager to study his own group first. Your organization will help you define the boundaries within which you will need to operate.

Just like the coach, the manager must expand the development of the team to include all aspects of the team's competition, including analysis of the opponent. However, there is one imposing difference between most work groups and a sports team: in sports, the opponent normally appears as an external foe. In the workplace, the opponent may not always appear as direct competition. Quite often, it's not so obvious for teams to identify who their opponent is. To answer the question of "who is your opposition?" just ask yourself, "What are we trying to accomplish? Who are we trying to please? What's stopping us? Who or what is working against us? What forces are resisting us?"

The "opposition" is everything that comprises your overall challenges and goals. It's everything that you're up against. In the business world, we need to spend some time understanding who or what our opposition is. It may be as obvious as another company or a competing product. Or it could be a product design challenge. Or a manufacturing quality problem. The opponent could be as subtle as the challenges of launching a new service initiative. Or how about the culture of an organization that you're trying to change? It could be something or someone that is not even in opposition to us, such as direct customers or customer departments within the same company. It could be totally inanimate, such as the obstacles in the way of reaching quantitative goals. The point is that if it's in the way of you achieving your goals and objectives, then it is an opponent. If it is an opponent, then you must defeat it to win. But first, regardless of who or what the opponent is, you cannot conquer what you do not know.

As in sports, the need exists for in-depth analysis of the opponent in business. Obviously, if an organization could spend great quantities of time engaged in thorough dissection of opponents, strategies, and plans, the benefits would be significant. Unfortunately, time never cooperates. Product tests, mathematical analyses, and role-playing exercises take time. Who has time to simulate the activity when they're too busy doing it? The point should not be lost, however, that there is no plan that will ever be created that could not benefit from even the shortest session of "what-ifs" with the players who will be counted on to carry it out.

Once, while working at a joint venture between a Japanese and U.S. automaker, I learned a lesson from one of the Japanese managers. He bragged that American companies spend "25 percent of the time planning and 75 percent of the time executing and fixing mistakes. In contrast, the Japanese companies spend 75 percent of the time planning and only 25 percent executing." I watched how natural it was seemed for the Japanese to question everything, and once they had the answers, they would question it some more.

I once walked in on a number of manufacturing process engineers designing a new manual assembly operation. They began brainstorming about all of the things that could possibly go wrong with this job. They were planning for the human being to fail. In effect, they had identified their opponent, in this case human imperfection in the form of the employee standing along the assembly line. This led them to design fail-safe error-proofing to protect against it. "What if the operator forgets to put a bolt in?" one asked. "What if he doesn't tighten it?" added another. That ignited a totally different brainstorming session, which resulted in designs for electronic sensors to tell if the operator reached into the box of bolts or not and whether his tool properly tightened the bolt. This was typical of their plans—always built with contingencies. They took the time to learn their opposition, and they tailored the way they worked accordingly.

If you have taken time to grasp the challenge in front of you, then why not "practice" against it? If you have studied and identified the obstacles, then you had better have contingency plans for every one of them. When the Allied forces attacked Normandy on D-Day to begin the end of World War II, they had contingencies for every obstacle and barrier that the Germans had built into the beachhead. Special equipment was built and air dropped. Tools were created, explosives modified, and troops trained for specific tasks. The triumph is well-known. What is less known is that the Allied forces had launched a similar attack earlier that year in Dieppe. At that time, with little knowledge of the German defenses and, as a result, few plans to counteract any of them, the mission ended with the slaughter of the Allied soldiers involved. The lessons learned—insight into the opposition's tactics and the observations of their own weaknesses—all helped steer the Allied forces to a winning plan in the end.

Opportunities to modify game plans and teach new approaches aren't always tied to such defined events. Leading an organization through change is a common scenario in which business leaders can make these kinds of preparations. If the challenges are well-known and documented, it is possible for managers to anticipate the reactions of employees and make plans to address their responses. Questions are easier to handle if you have prepared a list of answers to potential questions.

PUTTING THE LESSON IN ACTION

While I was managing a large assembly operation, we were faced with a projected drop in sales for one of our product lines. We would have to reduce output by 21 percent. Well, on a large assembly line, the only way to do that is to slow the line down and consolidate jobs. In our industry, that's called "rebalancing production." We decided to do it in two steps, separated by three months time. We went into the first reduction with a simple plan to rebalance the assembly line. We would be moving equipment, work stations, material containers and, in the end, eliminating some jobs. It was pretty standard stuff, I was told. So we quickly moved forward with putting together the new jobs and making the changes. Our engineers and managers pulled it all together and began to implement it.

Unfortunately, it was anything but "standard stuff." Everything that could go wrong did. It went horribly! We encountered safety problems, which were created from poor layout of the work area. We had problems getting our assemblers to perform their tasks in the allotted time, since they were struggling to make our jobs work. There were problems with equipment, parts, you name it. And amidst all of that, there were some pretty upset people. The manpower reduction was an emotional issue for the workforce. This only served to incite them. Everywhere, there were problems that we hadn't taken into account when we set up the new routines. And amidst all of the chaos, there were good, honest people trying to do a good job while they struggled with our poorly planned changes.

It took weeks to sort all of it out, and our inefficiencies cost us money. After a month of pure hell, things started settling down. I kept dreading that we would have to do it all over again in just a few months time. One of the managers turned to me and said, "Wow, if this first reduction was this bad, I wonder what the second one will be like?" The thought then occurred to me that we didn't need to "wonder what it would be like." We knew what it would be like. That's when I realized that we had just met our "opponent." This event—the rebalance of an assembly line—was our opponent. I told the staff that "We lost the first game, but we're playing the same team again in a few months." We were going to have to learn to play against our opponent. We had to adjust our plan, based on this "loss." However, in order to do that, we first needed to understand how we lost.

"Okay, group, what did we do wrong this time?" I asked them, as we sat around the conference table. (Obviously, this self-analysis isn't easy for a group to dive into.) There was nothing but silence at first. Nobody was going to step forward and say, "I screwed up." So I figured it may as well be me. And so I began. I set out to create an open forum that would be non-threatening. I openly discussed some of the wrongful assumptions I had made, as well as some poor decisions. I listed these on a large flip chart. I then asked for input from the group on how I should act differently the next time. (That got them going—the chance to tell the boss how to act!) From that point on, I was surprised. The discussion took off, and everyone became involved in assessing their actions. I'm sure that hearing the boss take shots at himself had an impact on some of them. They jumped right into the discussion, offering up accounts of their own mistakes and oversights. Since it was a focused activity, it didn't take long to complete.

That was the first step. Next we had to look at what we would do differently and how we would do it. Armed with the knowledge we gained from the original experience, it was easy to identify the challenges we would face next time. We created a detailed list of all the modified actions we would take, as well as all of the contingency responses we'd be prepared to enact. It was pretty impressive. The group sat back, nodding their heads, "Yeah, if we do this, we can win easily." Their level of preparedness was quickly motivating the group. It was a refreshing feeling of confidence. But our preparation didn't stop there. We were ready to practice our new plan.

So, with the plan in hand, we began to simulate various situations. We played out the series of "what if's" together, trying to anticipate arguments or obstacles that would be thrown at us. "Remember what happened last time on that particular job. What if that happens again?" I would hear from corners of the conference room. We checked our plan against these scenarios and determined additional responsibilities as contingency plans. We studied the behavior of various individuals and groups who had reacted negatively. Anticipating these conflicts ahead of time enabled us to talk them through. In the end, everyone was comfortable with what we could expect and how we would react. Not only had we developed a good game plan, but we also had practiced executing it mentally and as a team.

In the end, our second effort was an amazing success. Our first effort had lasted more than ten weeks. The second time around, we achieved all of our objectives in three days!

CHAPTER 9

Practice Is As Important As the Game

THE WILL TO WIN IS IMPORTANT, but the will to prepare is vital.

— JOE PATERNO
FOOTBALL COACH, PENN STATE

THE COACH'S LESSON

The Detroit Rockies was a collection of competitors, each trying to surpass the other. They loved to play and absolutely hated to practice. Their love of playing and their preference for live scrimmages during practice were based on their desire for full-speed, full-contact competition. They would rather do than plan. They wanted to skate instead of concentrating on a chalkboard's diagrams. Action was preferred over thought alone. So their reaction to drills and set, practiced formations was always one of disappointment.

Unfortunately for them, practices were a necessity. They had a lot to learn to eventually come together as a team. And they weren't going to learn these lessons unless I could spend quality time with them in an open learning environment. When I looked at the times when the kids were actually learning, I realized that they weren't gaining as much from games as one would think. Realizing that the practices were more valuable to our team's development, I tried to alter the routines and intensity of our practice sessions. My challenge was to create an environment where they would enjoy it or, at least, tolerate it.

I tried to treat practices very professionally, demanding attention and concentration. I arrived at each practice session with a plan detailing all of the drills and the amount of time to spend on each. I shared these plans with the players, hoping that they would realize that Coach Rob's practices were going to be more serious than what they were used to. We would work through all of our exercises and then take a few minutes to review the purpose and benefit of each; that way they didn't seem so rote or unnecessary to the players. And there was always positive, reflective encouragement on our progress. At every moment of the practice, I wanted there to be no mistake that what we were doing was learning and getting better.

Formality and structure, of course, is not what teenaged boys are looking for, at least not in our case. So I had to be careful that there was still some time for fun and informality. Knowing that they all had energy and personality that loved to come out on the ice, I would ease our way into practice by letting them have the first ten minutes of every hour to play around with the pucks however they wanted. I encouraged games of shinny, an old Canadian pond hockey game where one player grabs the puck and tries to score while all the other players chase him, trying to do the same. I goaded them into one-on-one challenges with each other. We joked a little more. I let them wrestle when they wanted to (or needed to). For that period of time, they had fun. Since the remainder of the practice would be more structured and disciplined, it was important for them to have their time and be themselves. I didn't want them to despise practice.

To maintain a close relationship with all of the players throughout their development, I strove to make individual contact with each player regularly. I started to spend more time one-on-one with players, while the others practiced drills. I tried to spend five to ten minutes a week with each player alone just to work on his own skills. We might move over to the side boards, or take over one end of the ice to do whatever it was we agreed he needed to work on. It was his lesson. Often, a player would start by saying, "I was thinking all week of what I should work on with you and I thought..." I could tell that they appreciated this attention and looked forward to working on something that would help them get better. I always believed that this method gave them selfish reasons to want to come to practice.

Attempting to instill more competition into the practices, I began to employ the regular use of drills in which head-to-head competition was involved. I, of course, was looking for the players to push themselves and each other. They were looking for the chance to compete against one of their buddies, leading ultimately to momentary bragging rights. So I would put them in situations directly against other players, while encouraging them to use tactics that I had taught them. By hyping the successful players and pulling aside the less victorious for remedial lessons, I was able to combine their desire and my own. Since I was a defenseman in my playing days, I would regularly challenge all the players to one-on-one competition against me. Their eyes lit up at the chance to beat the coach. A few times, in order to really stoke their competitive fires, I would offer $5 to anyone who got around me and scored on the goalie. Again, I would always offer individual pointers to all the failed attempts, and reinforcement (and $5) to the successful ones.

Of course, the lessons from each practice always had to be tied into the overall game plan. I always took opportunities to reinforce the relationship between what we learned in practice to what we applied in games. When we began to start winning, I would end each post-game talk and begin each practice with examples of good application of what we had learned. So as the boys began to no longer despise practice, they also started realizing the importance of it.

Play Like You Practice

"You play like you practice." The sooner a coach learns this lesson, the better. No team can ever hope to improve if it relies only on games to learn. Consider that in football, practices outnumber games by a significant ratio of about 6:1, more if you include preseason. Considering those numbers, you start to realize why famous coaches recognize that each player's character is shaped on the practice field.

A practice presents the team with the prospect of learning in a controlled environment. That's utopia for a coach. The coaching staff has everyone's complete attention for the entire time. No crowds, no interruptions, no pressure, no drama unfolding. Just a team drilling itself and testing its preparedness for the next opponent. A true teaching coach, one who thrives on developing and growing a team, values practices since they have so few boundaries for learning.

A coach has to get a team to think as one unit and to think in the same manner when it comes to playing the game. They have to embrace a game plan as their own and strive to execute it well. They need to know it thoroughly and be able to interpret it as a game changes. Players need to know what their role is and towards what end they must strive. In a game, they must be able to do all of this without the coach talking to them. This development is one of the most important functions of regular practice sessions.

That's why practices are key to developing players' understanding of the team game and the overall game plan. In practices, elements of the game plan are drilled over and over. Players run the same patterns many times, and then stand back to watch their teammates execute the same. Throughout this, the coaches are interacting with the players, reinforcing the same messages. In the meeting rooms, plays are sketched out on blackboards and reinforced as part of the overall plan. This degree of detail is constantly repeating itself.

Practice is the only situation in which a team can experiment and make mistakes without incurring a penalty or loss. Mistakes are necessary for any learning organization. Mistakes, however, are wasted unless they result in lessons learned. Therefore, if a player approaches practice with an indifferent attitude, a mistake will create no resulting change. For this reason alone, a team should strive to generate an intense, competitive atmosphere in the practices.

Since this practice time is precious to a teaching coach, the players must come to each practice willing to learn. This requires that the players listen to and internalize the lessons with the kind of intensity that they bring to a game. When executing drills or plays, they have to strive for the same level of perfection that will be required at game time. Realistically, it's not easy for coaches to get players excited about practice. However, it is possible to get players excited about improving themselves. It is a terrific source of motivation for them.

Consider for a moment the professional bodybuilder. Day after day, he or she lifts weights. Boring? Perhaps. Less exciting than competitions?

Certainly. So how do bodybuilders get excited about what they do day in and day out? They work out in front of mirrors. Everyday, they see themselves growing stronger, looking better. They see progress, and it excites them. And it brings them back the next day with that same excitement. They experiment. They try to lift more pounds than they've ever done before. There's excitement inherent to those kinds of personal challenges.

Just like the bodybuilder getting excited over progress, players need to feel progress, too. In this case, the coach has to hold up the mirror to the team. Both individuals and the entire group have to feel as if they're growing stronger, better, more proficient. They need to be shown or reminded of how they've improved. This reinforcement of positive growth only adds to self-confidence, makes them feel good about what they're doing, and keeps them coming back for more.

Likewise, it's important to allow the competitive spirit to flourish in practice. A team needs to be challenged during practices, both individually and as a group. Competition, friendly or otherwise, will encourage concentration and entice players to challenge themselves, as well as each other. Players who challenge each other in practice will only make each other better over the long run. Where a competitive spirit doesn't exist, coaches should encourage it. Drills that pit player against player in competitive situations can contribute to a competitive environment, as well as positive reinforcement to performers. Many coaches penalize poor intensity in practices with reduced playing time in games. Imagine how much more focus a group has when the intensity level in practice is raised.

Consider the 1997 Michigan Wolverine football team. A few weeks before the New Year's Day Rose Bowl game, the intensity had risen in practice so high that after one particularly physical exchange during a drill, a fight broke out between two senior players. The rest of the team watched in amazement. The Wolverines went on to win that Rose Bowl and a share of the National Championship. Afterwards, many interviewed players and coaches pointed to that episode as an example of how intensely focused their team was. One sophomore player said that when he saw two seniors hitting each other as if they were enemies, he realized that he needed to "raise his level of practice up a notch."

Lesson from a Legend: Pat Riley

 Under Pat Riley's tenure as head coach, the Los Angeles Lakers of the NBA were arguably the most dominant team of the '80s. With Hall of Fame stars such as Kareem Abdul Jabbar and Earvin "Magic" Johnson on their team, they had won championships in 1980, 1982, and 1985. Upon the start of the 1985–86 season, *Sports Illustrated* suggested that these Lakers could possibly be the greatest pro basketball team of all time.

Throughout that season, the team seemed to cycle between periods of great success and embarrassing failure. With players openly asking, "How do we top what we accomplished last year?" Riley faced a continuous challenge of maintaining intensity. "Anytime you stop striving to get better, you're bound to get worse. There's no such thing as simply holding on to what you've got," Riley would later observe about his team at that time.

During a mid-season practice, Riley decided that he had had enough and targeted his frustration on one of his star players. To the coach's amazement, the player replied, "I only got so much use left in my legs, and I'm not going to use it up in practice. I'm a game player." Having never encountered the challenge of trying to motivate some of the best talent ever to be combined on one team, Riley struggled all season. He could not seem to light a fire under them. His players thought that they could simply "turn it on" when it really counted. One player, when asked why he only appeared to play hard when the team seemed in danger of losing, smiled and said, "See me in March." He believed that nothing really mattered until playoffs.

Riley learned the lessons and documented them in his book *The Winner Within*. Unfortunately, the lessons of complacency came too late to salvage the 1985–86 season. The Lakers showed signs of fatigue throughout their playoff run. They had lost the edge to their game that comes from intense practice, as well as the physical conditioning that results from a commitment to preparation. When the Lakers players tried to "turn it on," it didn't happen. Riley recalls, "The holding back during the regular season had put us out of playoff condition. Playing below their potential had become an ingrained habit. The 'on' switch wasn't connected." As a result, the Lakers lost a championship. However, after heavy reflection, they learned a valuable lesson about the importance of preparation.

The Coach as Manager: Look for Learning Opportunities

Every organization must create learning opportunities if it hopes to improve. In business, these opportunities happen all the time. It's too bad that most managers don't realize it. Like a sports team, our work teams have practices more often than you think. Consider what a practice is for a sports team. It's a group activity where the game plan is discussed, drilled, and rehearsed. It's an opportunity for learning and development. It's the same for businesses. Those needs exist. And so do the practices.

The practice session for an organization can take many forms. It may be regular staff meetings. It could be product-testing exercises or market research. It could happen in a conference room or in the field. The only necessity of a practice is the existence of an opportunity for you to gather the members of a team for discussion or lessons. Remember that a practice session is a time when a coach or manager can help individuals develop personal skills, while bringing the entire team to a collectively higher level of performance. When put in this manner, it becomes apparent that the opportunities for a manager to teach and develop the team occur every day.

It's easy to grasp the significance of learning opportunities in the workplace if managers first realize that their employees are working independently most of the time. For that reason, it is imperative for team members to be focused in a common direction, following a unified overall strategy, and utilizing similar processes, techniques, and tools. The manager must create this uniformity. This is a difficult challenge when you consider that many managers don't normally spend much time with subordinates, let alone all of them collectively. So the manager must grab the opportunity to teach, develop, and lead the team any time he or she can.

This effort will begin with the game plan and be carried out by the common understanding and execution of it by the team members. In between those ends will be countless hours of coaching. There should be regular reinforcement of the same message. Individual lessons should always be related to the overall plan. Each individual role should be understood by all so that their interrelationships can be supported. There should be consistent discussion of overall goals and objectives, with regular reference to the game plan and the individual assignments that will help deliver the goals and objectives. Any opportunity to teach must be capitalized upon.

As the sports team practices in anticipation of the upcoming game's events, so too must the business team. The individual actions and assignments must be studied by the team members and coaching staff constantly. It is imperative for everyone to develop a deep understanding of the executables, so that mistakes can be avoided ahead of time.

The manager should create an environment that encourages attention to detail, a task that is difficult to generate in the heat of battle. Good managers will scrutinize timelines for details and deadlines. They will challenge unsupported statements or assumptions. Questions will be asked, and hypotheses will be offered. A product's failure will be discussed prior to it ever being built and sold. A market survey will be dissected from all angles before conclusions are drawn from the results. Teams will be as proactive in the planning stages as they are reactive after a disaster has occurred.

Once a group reaches this depth of understanding about the game plan, they can become a part of the process to modify it, or even create portions of it. They can challenge the previously laid plans. They should question each other's thinking. In a team environment, one person's plan can become a team effort after discussion. When employees engage in this type of analysis with managers who are willing to consider and possibly implement new suggestions, employees become more attached to results, and a better effort ensues. One will be surprised at how this exercise pushes individuals to make certain that their work is well-supported and without reproach. Of course, any group that continually challenges each other will only become stronger as a whole, as long as it's a healthy challenge. It's up to the manager to maintain group discussion on a nonpersonal level, and to establish that there are no bad ideas or questions.

PUTTING THE LESSON IN ACTION

In an attempt to re-create the practice sessions that I was using so well in the hockey arena, I looked for learning opportunities at work. I needed to find practice time. Looking at our activities as a team, it became pretty clear. I realized that the leadership group of our business unit was only getting together for staff meetings weekly. That was the only "team" time. This management team was comprised of production, quality, maintenance, and various representatives from the engineering groups, so it was important for them all to be working towards common goals. Since these weekly meetings were the only true "team" activities where they were all together, I would have to create new opportunities.

I began to have informal meetings three times a week with the leadership group to discuss our overall game plan. These sessions were meant to be gatherings where we would talk about our ongoing activities and discuss future plans, but they also allowed me to put it all in the context of our overall game plan. At these sessions, the game plan was the only focus, and the leaders of the group heard constant reinforcement of our plan.

These sessions became our "practices," and the time spent away from each other was "game time." Therefore, I wanted these meetings to teach, prepare, and focus the group so that when they went out and interacted with subordinates, they were speaking the same language and working towards the same goals. This activity would help build the foundation for a unified and cohesive approach to all of our initiatives.

At these regular meetings, we focused on our performance and adherence to the game plan. We followed a format that mimicked our game plan. I always began with an effort to establish focus for the group, referring to our overall vision and goals. We would review our performance to one of our quantified objectives. Then we would follow through with a status discussion of all the methods and systems that we had put in motion to achieve our stated objective. We would discuss progress and suggest changes or modifications. We would review action items that were in the form of individual assignments. Each employee involved would then give a summary of his or her execution of assigned tasks.

As a group, we had already set our overall goals and quantified our objectives. We had identified and prioritized our overall actions and translated them into assignments that directly supported them. In our conference room, we posted and tracked all of the measurements that were important to the objectives. We kept our eye on these "gauges" constantly. We questioned plans, created hypothetical situations, and brainstormed every planning opportunity we could.

By keeping these meetings informal, I maximized the amount of interaction that occurred. I needed every person there to gain an understanding of each other, as well as each other's functions. Like my hockey players, I wanted all my managers to understand each other's roles and how they were related to the same overall goals. So everyone got a chance to talk. Often, our discussions would take off on tangents. Someone might get on a roll talking about one of his or her initiatives. I would make certain that every individual had a chance to speak, usually by prompting the quiet ones to give updates on projects or issues to the group.

In the process, they learned about each other and about the roles each played in the overall plan. I remember once hearing a member of the production management leadership remark that she didn't realize that the industrial engineering department was working as hard as they were. "I always thought they had easy jobs, dreaming up silly things for us to implement," she said. "I didn't realize just how much detail goes into what they do."

As our direction and plans continued to mature, this meeting became ever more important. It was in this forum that I was able to constantly reinforce our direction. To keep these meetings brief, we limited the session to one hour in length. To avoid monotony, we selected only one objective per meeting to discuss, rotating through them all over the course of the month. Given that the meetings happened regularly, there wasn't too much that any one person could do that wasn't immediately compared to our overall strategies.

With the increased amount of interaction among members of the management team, we developed better plans and executed them with fewer mistakes. I believe this strategy helped to develop team ownership of issues that originally belonged to only one person. Our initiatives were now **team** initiatives. Our problems were **team** problems. Everyone's business was literally everyone's business. By creating the team context for all issues, everyone developed a vested interest in each other's work. It was extremely difficult for anyone to leave the room and go back to his or her tasks without knowing what the top priorities were for our operation.

STATUS MEETING FORMAT

Establish Focus

1. Review vision, goals, and objectives.
2. Review performance objectives.

Update Methods/Systems

NOTE: Before each meeting, decide what methods you will focus on. To save time, you may only want to focus on those processes that are problematic, are at a critical point, are critical to a key objective, and have not been updated recently.

For each method/system discussed:

1. Remind team how method fits in with overall objectives/goals.
2. Remind team of system roles.
3. Update status.
4. Assess effectiveness related to achievement of objectives.
5. Highlight any successes. Compile a list of actions that had a positive impact on performance/results.
6. Identify problems, mistakes, and causes.
7. Brainstorm solutions/lessons learned.

Discuss Other Successes, Challenges, or Issues

1. Provide each team member with an opportunity to share any other successes, challenges, and issues.
2. Allow time to brainstorm solutions to any problems or lessons learned from recent mistakes.

Identify Action Items

1. Select solutions that are most appropriate.
2. Identify action plan for each solution and lesson learned.
3. Make assignments for each action plan.

Reestablish Focus

1. Identify milestones for next time period.
2. Remind team how these fit with overall goals and objectives.

CHAPTER 10

Every Player Must Have a Role

AN AUTOMOBILE GOES NOWHERE EFFICIENTLY unless it has a quick, hot spark to ignite things, to set the cogs of the machine in motion. So I try to make every player on my team feel he's the spark keeping our machine in motion. On him depends our success.

— KNUTE ROCKNE
FORMER FOOTBALL COACH, NOTRE DAME

THE COACH'S LESSON

When I took over the Detroit Rockies, I first had to learn each player's personality and abilities to help determine what role he would play. Given the limited number of kids playing at the arena, I didn't have the option of replacing any of the players, so I would have to use them all somehow. As it turned out, I had quite a few "wanna be a star" players, along with a few legitimate ones. Too many of the guys wanted to make the big play. There was never enough ice time for them. Most importantly, they wanted to score the goals. In the dressing room after the games, goal scorers displayed all the cockiness that one night's worth of heroics could generate. And they lived for that.

Unfortunately, being on a team required many other roles for them. They were not all going to be the goal scorers. Obviously, one of the hardest lessons some players had to learn was to accept the role that the team needed them to play. It took all of three years to finally get them to think in a team mode.

In teaching them to act and play like a team, I had to do some pretty drastic things. I was harsh on players who chased after the puck and left their positions to do it. In the dressing room after the games, I would chastise any player who acted selfishly, *especially* if he scored a goal. (You could imagine the looks on their faces. Flush with a lack of understanding, they would stare at me, wondering if they had heard me correctly. After all, "Aren't we supposed to score goals, coach? Isn't that how we win?") My stern reprimands would include words like "selfish" and straddle accusations of "not caring about your teammates." I never tolerated complaints about ice time, either, whether they came from the players or, more often, their parents. People played according to the need for their role at the time, their overall team play, and whether I was satisfied with their efforts in games or in practice.

If we were going to win, they had to learn to play a team game. So they learned about each piece of the puzzle first, and then how the pieces all fit together. They learned about the assignments that, although not as desirable as scoring goals, had to be carried out in order to win games. They had to learn how to fight off defenders in the corners, or how to check an opposing player. I always overemphasized the importance of the less glamorous roles. I talked about the importance of the "grinders" and the "grunts" more than I ever talked about the offensive roles. Of course, this totally blew their collective minds. I was taking away all of the glamour of the game. It was as if "the coach" didn't appreciate the goal scorers. The truth was that I did appreciate every single role that had to be played. What I needed, however, was to share that appreciation with the players. So I decided to try a little role reversal during practices.

I began to switch assignments on players over the next few practices. It was instructive to have players play in positions that they weren't used to. The star center found that playing defense wasn't that easy. After a while, he better understood where a defender should be on the ice and why. This gave the players exposure to all the roles that their teammates had to play. Eventually, they understood that the team needed everyone. Someone had to fight for the puck in the corners. Someone had to backcheck hard. Someone had to play defensively against the opponent's big scorer. This role switching helped strengthen each player's understanding of the total game and gave them all a growing appreciation for each other.   Most of all, each individual had to learn to play within his own role. They had limitations that had to be respected. As I told them, it didn't mean they wouldn't improve or develop their capabilities. It just meant that if you're not the fastest skater with the sweetest moves in the arena, then you shouldn't be carrying the puck up the ice. If you're the defender then you shouldn't be standing in front of their net, trying to get into the play.

There Is a Role for Every Player

The title for this chapter could easily have been "There is a role for every player." The truth is that this statement fits both ways. Each player on the team must fit into a role, and each role must fit the player.

When we talk about roles, there are two aspects that are important: The first is the player's role while the team is on the playing field. The second is the individual person's role as a member of a team of people. They may sound similar, yet they are unique in their contribution to the team's dynamics.

As a player on the team, the role will involve assignments and tasks during the games. It may relate to protecting a certain area of the field or possibly defending against the opponent's star center underneath the basket. It is a role that has strategic value based on the design of plays.

These kinds of roles will be defined when the overall game plan and playing style are being developed. The need for that quick linebacker may not exist until the team develops game plays and defensive formations that require it. This only underscores the need for a well-thought out game plan prior to defining or making personnel changes. Without an overall vision of what kind of team a coach wants to have and a plan on how to get there, how can he determine what kind of player his team needs?

One should also keep in mind that these roles may change during various game situations. This is especially true if a team is forced to alter its game plan. An opponent may drive a team away from their game plan by successfully countering their actions. A college basketball team intent on playing man-to-man defense may get burned badly with pick plays and be forced to retreat to a zone defense.

Away from the playing field, however, the role takes on a different dimension. This role is more personal. It speaks more to the type of person the player is when among peers. Does the player fit the role of the team leader, for example? Or is he or she a player that refuses to give up, regardless of how much he or she is down? A team needs different types to fill out a well-balanced group of players. Teams may need some combination of different characteristics among the players, such as a sense of humor, energy, youthfulness, experience, etc. These are the personality traits that develop the good chemistry that helps a team develop and come together away from the playing surface. An experienced, poised player may play a role on the team by helping to create a professional, disciplined approach during team meetings or in the locker room.

Above all, it's important for the coach to identify the roles that need to be filled on the team. This bridges the gap between the overall vision of a game plan and the actual execution during games.

Unfortunately for some starry-eyed players, there are only so many positions on a team, and each one must be filled. Not everyone can be the starting quarterback or the clean-up hitter. Not every hockey player can be the leading scorer on the team. Not every basketball player can be the big rebounder under the boards. It's a team game, and each position has to be filled with the same level of importance.

A team cannot win on the back of one individual star. Find any team in sports that has a player who believes that he is *the* star, or who acts like he is *the* star, and you will probably find a team that is divided and lacks unity. Selfishness does not go far with teammates in sports.

In fact, a team that is comprised of players who all *want* to be the star has a high likelihood of failing. Those players will be far more likely to only look for their own opportunities. They will measure their success in terms of their own gains. How many teams with rosters filled with high priced "prima donnas" have failed in the past?

But the roles for players go far beyond basic positions. A team's various roles also involve each player's special abilities. Each team needs a diverse combination of qualities in its players. Raw, high-scoring, natural talent is needed, but so is gritty, fight-for-every-chance effort. Coaches want players who can do the dirty work. Better yet, coaches yearn for players who will do the dirty work *and* want to do it well.

Lesson from a Legend: John Wooden

 For all of the NCAA championships that John Wooden's UCLA Bruins won, you would believe that these teams must have been stocked with star players. While it's true that there were future NBA stars on those teams, there were not enough to explain ten national championships in twelve years. The truth is that there were many Bruins who were not as memorable as Kareem Abdul Jabbar and Bill Walton.

Wooden knew that everyone had a role to play. It might not be as glamorous as others, but it was necessary all the same. Hand in hand with that necessity was the need to make players feel appreciated. In Wooden's words, "I tried to let them know they were important, that they were valued. All members of the team are important. Each role is crucial."

Wooden was a constant proponent of team play. He developed players to fit into their roles, and nothing more. Sure, he drove them to perfect their preparation and to excel in their game performance. But above all, he taught them how to win as a group. Many former players talk about how Coach Wooden made every player feel important. One young center with terrific talent played most of his college career as a back-up to one of college basketball's greatest centers, Bill Walton. As a new recruit, Coach Wooden explained to this young man that his role would be to challenge Walton in practice every day. If he did that, by the time he graduated, he could become the *second* best center in college, help UCLA win, and go on to have a successful professional career. Eventually, after consecutive national crowns, Swen Nater graduated out of his understudy role and stepped into his first professional year with San Diego of the American Basketball Association (before it joined with the NBA) and won Rookie of the Year.

With all of the fanfare that UCLA received, there were usually large gatherings at the post-game press conferences. Wooden recalls that the reporters were fairly predictable in their attention to the actions of players like Jabbar, Walton, Gail Goodrich, and Walter Hazzard. This narrow focus of praise ran counter to Wooden's own style. As a result, Wooden steered conversations away from the topic of his star performers, instead focusing on other players. Wooden now recalls, "I always tried to use this opportunity to praise those individuals the media would overlook. I would say, 'When I put so-and-so in just before the half and he made that steal, it quite possibly could have been the turning point in the game.' I wanted to let other players know they were very important to the team. I would be more likely to praise (star) players privately."

The Coach as Manager: Understanding the Role of Each Group Member

Trying to teach a group of employees how to play a "team game" is not easy for any manager. Employees are not always focused on the group's overall objectives as much as they are on their own. They have tasks to complete, and they would like to carry them out as smoothly and quickly as possible. This will enable them to go home to their families with as little stress as possible. True, it's fairly selfish, but it's only natural. The manager's challenge is to help establish the relationship between the employees' performance, that of their peers, and the potential overall success that should be beneficial to everyone.

So, like the sports team, the work group has roles that need to be played. The manager, upon defining the overall vision, purpose, and goals for the group, will define what is needed from the workforce. These roles will involve more than just the individual jobs. They may encompass support relationships, reporting structures, levels of audit, etc.

It's important for a manager to understand the entire scope of all the individual roles on the team. Too often, when defining the work assignments, managers stop after answering the "what will they do?" or "how will they do it?" This level of detail has to grow to include tougher questions such as "How will they support or interact with others?" or "What should they know or understand about the bigger picture to begin to think independently?"

We tend to underestimate the power of an organization of employees that is truly independent in their direction. This can only come from a true, deeper understanding of their roles and those of their peers. On the football field, a coach doesn't holler at a player to make specific moves, such as, "Turn right and run forward about six yards and then turn left." No, instead the coach calls the play and the player has a deep understanding of what his purpose is, where he should be, what to anticipate, and where his teammate is probably going to be. This is the level of understanding of their roles that we have to reach with our employees.

Fit Employees in Their Most Suited Roles

Employees have roles to play, just like sports players. And once again, these roles may differ drastically among individuals. In any organization, there will be jobs or assignments that will be viewed by some people as unfavorable. In the workplace, where you are dealing with egos, ambitions, and careers, people have their own ideas about which assignments or roles they want. An employee looking for the chance to lead or supervise others may object to a desk assignment that is heavy in data analysis. Many people jealously perceive other assignments as more preferable, which can lead to animosity towards the person in that desired position.

To maximize job satisfaction while leveraging employees' individual strengths, managers should strive to fit people with their most suited roles. This is ideal. Keep people happy and still get results. Unfortunately, it doesn't always work that way. Much to their disappointment, many employees are given assignments that they don't perceive as valuable. So how do you motivate someone by convincing them that they're making a valued contribution?

When the Team Wins, Everyone Wins

The challenge is to teach employees to view success in the context of the entire team winning. If an organization is successful, then all the players are winners. If the "grunts and grinders" share in the success and limelight equally with the "stars" then they are *all* part of that success and the trappings that come with it. This notion can't be stressed enough in the workplace! If a team at work achieves its goals and is rewarded, then all of the individuals who participated in the effort should share in that success. Every player on a championship team is a champion. It's the same for losing teams; seldom should any one employee get singled out for recognition when the organization as a whole is failing.

By teaching the group all of the roles that need to be executed in order to win, they will become familiar with what it will take for *all of them* to win. Showing them how everyone's responsibilities are interdependent will only underscore the importance of teamwork. After time, they may begin to respect each other's positions and view their own as integral to the overall achievements. Familiarity with each other's roles also helps create a team that watches out for each other. To the extent possible, employees should experience other jobs in their work team, such as through a methodical job rotation cycle. This action achieves more than just a cross-trained work-force. It helps expand the understanding each employee has of what it takes for the entire work group to succeed.

One-on-one conversations with employees are opportunities for managers to stress the criticality of each individual's role. Making time with dissatisfied employees to discuss details of what might be viewed by them as unglamorous work will only emphasize the importance of those details in the bigger picture. Ideally it will give the employee a greater sense of self-worth. It will also be an opportunity for a manager to stress the significance of the tasks to the overall success of the business team.

There is mileage to be gained by paying attention to the contributions that are made without fanfare. We should recognize day-to-day consistency and dependability as quickly as the Herculean accomplishments. If this is done in public, in front of the team, then it can only reinforce the value that everyone brings to the team. And it will help employees to understand in what ways others are contributing to the common cause.

PUTTING THE LESSON IN ACTION

In the workplace, I began to use the same approaches that I used on the ice. It was important for everyone to know and understand their roles, as well as the roles of their "teammates." If they were going to succeed as a team, then they needed to truly work together and function as a team.

I began to spend a lot of time with all levels of the organization, talking specifics about their different assignments and the importance of those assignments. Our talks, one-on-one, focused on their value as individual members of the team. "You may think you're just coming in every day and plugging away at your meaningless tasks," I would implore, "but what you don't realize, is that this team will fail if you don't perform your tasks, and perform them well. This team depends on you." This appeal for team concern was always framed in the context of "team success." I would always add, "You know that this team will not succeed unless we all succeed."

However, the personal plea is not enough. Individuals need to understand how they contribute and how their role directly supports other teammates, the game plan, and ultimately the results achieved. I made sure to spend time with as many individuals as my time allowed. I met regularly with members of my management staff, one at a time, to review the details and notes of their own plans. Showing them that their work was important enough for the "boss" to spend hours immersed in the details helped them feel noticed and appreciated. By avoiding questioning every detail and instead focusing on the overall game plan, I was always reemphasizing their role on the team.

When planning the execution of major undertakings, we always met as a group to discuss it. We used our standard meeting format, which was based on our approach to the game plan. Details were worked out in front of the entire team. Throughout this discussion, I walked the group through each individual assignment, encouraging the responsible person to add detail. This served to make the individual feel that his or her role was important, while educating the remaining team members about their peer's role. A typical conversation went like this: "Dan will be implementing the new product scheduling system next week and he will be working directly with our material delivery people. He will focus on loading correct model mixes into the process, so he's going to need some help from you folks in Quality to verify these parts as they move through the process. Dan, why don't you explain specifically what you'll be doing and what support you're going to need?"

This way all team members became familiar with the tasks that their companions were responsible for. Engineering became aware of the quality department's issues, while the maintenance folks understood the constraints that the production managers needed to work around. I wasn't looking to create redundancy or duplicate expertise. I just wanted to raise awareness. Pretty soon, they were reminding each other of dates, deadlines, and forgotten duties. On one occasion, I was surprised to hear a maintenance manager chime in on a product engineering concern, "Hey, Sally, you'll need to remember to let Financial know how many parts you end up with so they can make a cost adjustment. Remember, we forgot that last time." The team began to relate to each other in a way that they never had before. I would always commend this type of behavior, describing it as the act of what had become a "true team." Enthusiasm was contagious, even for the tasks that had no glory in them at all but that served a purpose to the team.

Of course, knowledge was contagious, too. I took pride in the fact that any member of the leadership team of my operation was equally versed in all aspects of our business. Any one of them could answer for work that one of the teammates was doing. That kind of appreciation for each other's work raised the level of confidence to new heights.

CHAPTER 11

Coach the Team, Coach the Unit, Coach the Player

Effectively managing players requires more than just ensuring everyone understands the game plan, practices hard, and plays well on game day. It must also include an acute appreciation of the fact that each player is an individual—with specific needs, interests, and perspectives.

— Bill Walsh
FORMER HEAD COACH, SAN FRANCISCO 49ERS

THE COACH'S LESSON

I had developed the Detroit Rockies into a team that played with an aggressive style. We were fast and we were physically tough. Our game plan was based on playing with a high level of intensity and speed while in the opposing team's end of the ice. One key to that plan was to use aggressive forechecking, which is a tactic of rushing at a team in their end when they have control of the puck, attempting to force them to turn it over so that we can gain control. We specialized in this, since it could be supported by our two best attributes: speed and physical toughness. Since we could force opponents to make mistakes in their end, our plays were designed for quick transitions after turnovers by the opposing team.

With our game plan in hand, the team had to learn how this type of approach worked. Starting with the basics of simple positioning and movement, we began to develop their understanding of this method. These lessons were given in front of blackboards, as well as on the ice in slow motion drills. The assistant coaches and myself spent hours coaching the players and running them through drills. We practiced forechecking formations and worked on taking quicker, one-timed shots at the net. Our fast-paced style of play would be based on our success in executing these plays. All of this was aimed at getting the entire team to a common level of understanding and preparedness.

On a lower level, I had one specific line on the Rockies that would have an assignment with a few variations. This playing unit, my "grind line" as I used to call them, consisted of three guys that were very good defensively. They would often be used to play against an opposing team's best offensive line, since they could defend against them better than our other lines. While the "grind line" wasn't very proficient at scoring themselves, they were extremely effective at keeping the other team from scoring. This threesome could easily learn and apply our new forechecking approach; however, they were not as adept at handling the puck when they forced a turnover. So their lessons were somewhat different. While I coached them to play with the same aggressive style when attacking the other team, they would attack differently so that they could better get in position to defend against the opposing line if we lost control of the puck. This allowed them to return back to our end zone in a position to defend against opposing players. This lesson was unique to them based on their purpose. The other lines didn't need that lesson since it didn't pertain to their roles.

As I taught this defensive line their variations to our plan, there were a few distinct tasks and assignments that the individuals would have to learn. On that particular line, one player's role had him often fighting for control of the puck in the corners. He needed specific training on controlling the puck with one hand and using his body as leverage while fighting off an opposing player along the boards. This took one-on-one time with him to help him develop this technique. Eventually, the team was trained on their overall game plan, the methods and systems we would use, and the specific tasks they would execute.

Don't Forget the Playing Unit

Normally, when we think of a team, we envision a group of people working together towards a common goal. With that singular focus, we tend to deal with the entire group as a whole. Too often, a coach only concentrates on coaching the team. As strange as this may sound, the team exists, and therefore must be coached, on many different levels. The team is really comprised of three, interrelated yet separate entities: the whole team, the playing unit, and the individual player. These three entities exist on every team, sports or otherwise.

The concept of the entire team as one of the entities is fairly understandable. It's the entire group of players working together to execute a game plan with a well-balanced and focused group performance. Likewise, the concept of the individual player as an entity is also self-explanatory. However, the notion of the playing unit may be new to some.

The playing unit is the group of players who are assigned to play together to execute certain plays or handle various situations. While comprised of individuals and part of the entire team, it is this small group that must work directly together and are most impacted by each other's actions. In football, the playing unit might be the defense. While part of the larger team, their tasks and challenges are distinctly different than their teammates on the offense.

Smaller sub-groups may exist, as well. On the defensive playing unit, the defensive front linemen would be considered a playing unit as well, since their tasks are all related and distinctly different from those of the linebackers and defensive backs standing behind them. Regardless of how many smaller playing units can be defined, the point still remains that there is a living, breathing entity that exists between the level of individual player and team. As such, playing units have needs that are unique to them.

These three units are similar yet different in their training needs, their preparation, and their game focus. It's essential that a coach differentiate between the needs of each of these entities because the team has to be able to perform at each of these levels in order to succeed. The individual player must excel with her assigned tasks and assignments. Her efforts must then mesh with those of her teammates on the playing unit. Lastly, all the actions of all the players must be in concert in order for a complete group effort to exist.

For example, a football team may be learning the run-and-shoot offense. This playing style will consist of many plays where the quarterback will take the snap, immediately scramble laterally towards the sideline with some of his blockers, and deliver a pass in another direction. To properly execute these plays, the entire offense will have to learn that particular approach to moving the football. More specifically, the offensive line will have to work separately on different blocking and movement patterns. On an individual level, the offensive guard will have to work on his lateral movement in order to get into position to block for the quarterback.

Since the tasks at each level are different, so too should be the lessons. Before embarking on creating lessons, a coach must first accept the notion that each entity has its own personality and its own needs. Not all lessons will be pertinent to each one. Two players may receive entirely different coaching, if their assignments or skill development needs require so. In keeping with the structure of the game plan pyramid, individual assignments and defined specific tasks will dictate what skills are needed to properly execute the assignments or tasks. In addition to skills, form will follow function for all support elements as well, such as motivation, physical environment, and team cooperation. So the playing unit's assignments and tasks will dictate their development and support needs. Likewise for the individuals that comprise the unit.

The one absolute that exists is that all lessons should fit into the overall game plan. That constancy helps to link the lessons together into one learning experience. A coach can never underestimate the impact on a player of seeing how each player's distinct lesson evolves from the same game plan. That common purpose needs to exist in every player's mind throughout his preparation.

Lesson from a Legend: Anson Dorrance

 Known for his disciplined and intense practices, Anson Dorrance has established his women Tar Heels soccer teams as some of the best prepared groups to ever take the field in NCAA play. However, Dorrance displays depth in his psychological understanding of the team dynamics that he must deal with. His teaching is aimed at reaching all three entities of the team.

While known for his close, personal relationships with his players, he has been successful in inspiring the Tar Heels to dip deep into the well of their potential and draw out the most possible. He understands that his female players are indeed different than the fellows he played with and coached at the University of North Carolina–Chapel Hill. He allows much more personal time and group interaction to occur as part of his efforts to bond the unit into a true team. He allows disagreements and personality conflicts to arise during intense moments, knowing that they will be settled by senior players and cooler heads.

The very structure of the practice week serves to develop all three entities of the team. During his regimented practice session, the activities are aimed at different units on different days. Normally, NCAA games are held on weekends with practices during the week. After allowing the team to take Mondays off to rest, the group reconvenes on the practice field on Tuesdays. Tuesdays are mainly reserved for fitness drills. These are obviously aimed at increased growth of personal physical capability. Less obvious is the focus on individual performance, which is the underlying theme for Tuesday.

Wednesday's practices are centered around both the individual and playing units. The team goes through one-on-one drills that put the players in situations where they can challenge themselves to try new tactics. In these drills, the Tar Heels hone their skills and test them out on each other. The remainder of the day is spent in small-sided drills. These put groups of players with or against other small groups—three forwards against two defenders and a goalie, for example. Wednesdays help move the focus from individual performance towards the small playing unit.

Two days before a game, the team plays a full-field scrimmage game. This day serves to recreate game-time situations, with the starters facing the reserves. Here, players are encouraged to apply what they have been working on alone and in small groups earlier in the week. It is imperative that these individual lessons be transferred into the overall team's development. These game-time simulations force the players to work together as a team in an environment where they can learn and be taught without consequences.

Finally, the day before a game, Dorrance keeps the practice light, with the emphasis on finishing drills. During these drills, Dorrance allows a greater amount of camaraderie to come out in place of the intensity apparent earlier in the week. Drills on this day are designed to keep the team relating to each other personally as much as they are about rehearsing passing and shooting plays.

Former UNC player and current U.S. team star Mia Hamm recalls how Dorrance's practice schedules reached all levels of the team throughout the week. In referring to his training regimen for the game weeks, Hamm says, "It was this progression from individual to team and back again that gave us an appreciation for how all the different parts can mesh together into one smooth-running machine."

The Coach as Manager: Identifying Business Units

For the manager, the business organization exists on different levels also. Regardless of his or her level of authority in the company, a manager should be able to look at the people reporting to him or her and identify, at the minimum, three levels of the team, and quite possibly more. This will be true for a chairman of a corporation or a warehouse supervisor. The initial step for a manager is to recognize the various entities within his or her span of control.

Once again, identifying the overall team, as well as the individual, is fairly straightforward. Identifying all the working units that may exist is more difficult. For a manager, this may be a combination of smaller groups, or subsets of the same group. It could be a department within an overall organization or a pair of payroll processing clerks. The individuals in this unit will have commonality in their purpose and, more than likely, in their professional requirements and developmental needs.

Like the sports team, the three different entities of the business team will have both common and different requirements when it comes to their professional development. As the overall plan is established for the organization, the needs of each level become more defined. Observations of these groups and individuals will round out further the developmental requirements. The entire team may need to understand the overall game plan, including aspects that may not totally affect them. The smaller working units will need to know and be adept at all the aspects of their function necessary for them to carry out their portion of the overall plan. Individually, a member of the team will need to be capable of performing specific tasks that are required for him or her to support the larger team and the team's goal. In all cases, the development and support needs will be defined as the game plan pyramid is completed.

Why is this such a big deal in the workplace? Quite often, in the course of day-to-day business, managers fail to treat equally all the various units at work in the organization. We may spend too much time managing the company or department, while not spending time developing and interacting with individuals. Or we may dedicate too much time to individuals and smaller work groups, but fail to bring it all together as an organization. In some cases, we may never even realize that multiple entities are alive and well in the same organization.

In larger companies, it's too easy to spend an inappropriate amount of time managing each level. Many managers may realize that they are:

➤ Spending little time with the entire group while only talking in vague terms.

➤ Spending some time with smaller work groups, but focusing only on goals.

➤ Spending too much time with only the individuals who are failing or are "problems."

Many managers don't realize that there is too much to lose by not teaching all three levels with an equal amount of time, effort, and detail. Even worse, managers can send each level separate messages that are not connected to the same strategy. How can people learn the roles that they need to execute in order to help their work group to achieve its goals? How can the work group understand how to play its role within the bigger organization? How can an entire organization succeed if it doesn't comprehend an overall strategy and how to carry it out?

PUTTING THE LESSON IN ACTION

In a manufacturing operation I managed a few years ago, our entire facility was striving to make some major improvements in cost, quality, and productivity. We were starting up a new product line and needed to staff it at the same time another product line was losing sales. We were pushing to reduce headcount in an effort to become competitive on the existing line, while redeploying the extra employees to the new line. This was a major undertaking that required a lot of organization and preparation.

As the game plan developed, it became obvious how the lessons and direction would be different for the various entities of my organization. And so I began to teach the team. The lessons began at a macro level to establish the overall strategy and style of execution. "What would we have to do?" and "In what manner would we have to do it?" To make productivity gains, we discussed specific actions and measures that we would have to undertake.

The reduction of employees was the tricky aspect, everyone agreed. Fortunately for us, the corporation was rolling out some new practices and techniques to use for exactly this type of activity. Among them was a unique process to analyze and streamline employees' work content. This tool could be used to study and improve the efficiency of any job: production, quality, even my own. In our game plan, this initiative would become one of the methods/systems we would use to help achieve our stated objective. Obviously, everyone had to know this. So I taught the entire team the new process so that we would all share the same approach to identifying productivity gains.

Within the team, the industrial engineers were the functional group that normally led any work analysis or job design. They quickly recognized that they would be key to the successful implementation of the new process. If they didn't support it and make it go, it simply wouldn't. As a result of their narrow scope, their lessons were focused on the details of the new process. They had to become proficient in the fine points of the process. They would need to understand it so well that they could explain it to the impacted employees. So, I pulled all the industrial engineers together as a functional group more often, in order to discuss at great length the process that they would lead. Their training was specific and their role clearly identified.

Of the industrial engineers, one in particular was having trouble with a certain aspect of the job. Since the process affected workers on the floor, the job involved interacting with groups of hourly, unionized employees and handling potentially difficult situations. This engineer needed to learn some basic skills that would help him to make presentations to large groups of employees who might not be receptive to the message. He needed specific assistance in preparing understandable presentations, facilitating difficult meetings, and diffusing conflict. As well as attendance at a few classes on these topics, his lessons came in the form of many one-on-one sessions where we reviewed his material, critiqued presentations, performed dry runs, and walked through some role-playing exercises.

The lessons were different, but they all shared a foundation in the same plan and were aimed at the same goal. Throughout the "coaching" of each level, I always tried to stress that the lesson was linked to each person's role, which was linked to the greater team's goal. By taking the task at hand, or the lesson of the moment, and explaining the interrelationship of it to the overall roles within the "team," I constantly reinforced our master game plan.

The Game Plan Pyramid—Skills through Team Cooperation

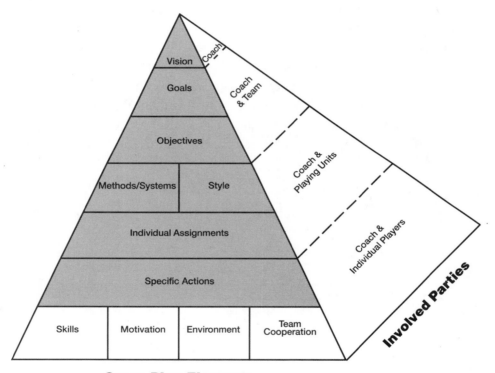

Game Plan Elements

How to Develop Your Players Into a Championship Team

SKILLS

➤ **Step 1: Identify skill requirements.**

For each process flow you developed in Coach's Playbook 1, list the essential skill requirements for each individual, as well as for the team as a whole. Be sure to:

❑ Be as specific as possible. The skill requirements you identify should:

___ Be observable.

___ Be targeted specifically to your team members' jobs (e.g., in addition to a general knowledge of tax laws and accounting, an accountant needs to know the specific payroll system and payroll schedule of his or her organization).

___ Include skills needed for your work units and your entire team to work well together (e.g., listening skills, communication skills, etc.).

___ Include both complex skills and fundamental skills (the "absolutely must do wells"). Don't assume that people know how to perform the basics.

➤ **Step 2: Prepare development plans.**

For each individual and work unit, as well as the team as a whole:

❑ Identify any skill gaps that exist (i.e., skills that are needed that don't already exist—again, don't forget to consider both basic as well as complex skills).

❑ List options for developing each of the deficient skills (e.g., coaching/ mentoring, training programs, on-the-job training, practice, role playing, simulations, etc.).

❑ Develop a skill-building plan for each individual and work unit, and for the team as a whole.

MOTIVATION AND ENVIRONMENT

➤ Step 1: Identify other barriers to performance.

For each individual, work unit, and team:

❑ Identify any motivational issues that might prevent your employees from meeting performance expectations. Ask yourself:

___ What might make people not want to do what is needed to execute the game plan?

___ What can be done to make them want to execute the game plan? To inspire them?

❑ Identify any environmental obstacles that might prevent your employees from meeting performance expectations (e.g., ergonomics, resources, equipment, authority, time, process, etc.)

❑ Plan strategies to address each motivational and/or environmental barrier you identify.

TEAM COOPERATION

➤ Step 1: Clarify performance expectations regarding team cooperation.

Your entire team needs to know exactly what your expectations are with respect to teamwork.

❑ Lead them in a visioning exercise by encouraging your team to share their thoughts and ideas about teamwork, describe potential obstacles that could prohibit them from working effectively together as a team, and offer suggestions for creating an environment of team cooperation.

❑ Once the visioning exercise is over, be sure to openly summarize your team's agreed-upon definition of team cooperation and the specific responsibilities each team member has in helping to achieve your team's common vision.

➤ Step 2: Create an environment of open communication.

To help pave the way toward true team cooperation, it's imperative that you establish an environment of trust, honesty, and fairness. The best way is by opening up a two-way stream of communication with your team members. You can do this by:

❑ Involving team members in planning and problem-solving activities.

❑ Providing each team member with individual airtime.

❑ Treating mistakes and problems as learning experiences.

❑ Being open about your own weaknesses and mistakes.

❑ Inviting constructive comments, opinions, and advice from team members.

❑ Keeping feedback and group discussions constructive and non-personal.

❑ Communicating "negative" feedback privately. Never chastise any individual in front of the group.

The Business of Winning

Section 3

Execute at Game Time

WINNING IS NOT A SOMETIME THING; it's an all the time thing. You don't win once in a while; you don't do things right once in a while; you do them right all the time. Winning is a habit.

— VINCE LOMBARDI

With a solid game plan—studied, practiced, and supported by individual roles and assignments—the team's focus now shifts to game-time execution. It's now time for the players to play. All the preparation leads up to this moment when plans are validated and players are tested. This is where the rubber hits the road.

While obvious in sports, game time does not carry a clear connotation in the world of business. There isn't always a definitive event for which the team has been preparing. However, upon closer scrutiny, game time exists every day.

Consider what a game really is. It is the moment when a team must deliver; it has to perform the executables. The team has planned and prepared for this moment. It cannot be interrupted once it has begun. And it must have the desired result in order for success to be at hand. It almost always impacts the team's eventual goal, and it usually involves the customers.

In other words, game time happens all the time. It could happen twelve times a day or twelve hundred times a day. In business, it is all the time.

There are many "game situations" in business. They can be intense, high-stress periods when a group is executing a plan that it has been working on for a long time: the launch of a new vehicle that has been four years in planning, the staging of a major entertainment event after months of preparation, the rollout of a major advertising campaign. Or it could be the everyday execution of a plan: serving the rush-hour traffic at the counter of a McDonald's restaurant, or service calls by the cable man. They happen often and, as such, must be executed flawlessly.

Mistakes suddenly take on heightened significance. In practices, mistakes can be accepted, if not tolerated. Mistakes are part of the learning process in the development phase, and can help a team identify areas for improvement. In games, however, errors must be minimized. Mistakes made in games may have significant repercussions. An improperly timed miscue can quickly change the direction of the game or, worse yet, the score.

For this reason, it is imperative that the entire team exercise self-control, discipline, and good judgment. This applies to coaches as well as players. They all must adhere to the game plan as closely as possible. Any variance to the plan during the game will normally be initiated by the coach. Of course, players must have the latitude to react to game situations, but not in a manner that jeopardizes the team's ability to execute the plan.

While the players shift their attention completely from preparation to execution, the biggest change in roles belongs to the coach. The coach's role as teacher and developer of players becomes subordinate. Game time is not the time for teaching; the coach must move to the background and let his team play. Waiting for opportunities to make personnel changes or to call different plays, the coach remains on the sideline or on the bench, observing from a distance. While watching mistakes and errors, he must balance his own desire to intercede with the team's need for the freedom and room to play their game. There is no place for micromanagement by the coach during a game.

This holds true in the workplace as well. Micromanagement, one of the biggest complaints of many employees about their boss, is a productivity-killer. It is a distraction to employees and often has the opposite effect of the intended result. Just as the coach has to stay on the bench while the players are executing the plan, so too must the manager. And it will be just as difficult for the manager to do.

Everyone has to stay focused and remember their assignments. **A team must play with discipline** in order for a game plan to be executed well. This discipline extends to the coach as he shifts his focus, as well. Recognizing that the coach's role changes at game time will allow him to comfortably settle into a role that is part observer, part director, part conductor, and part cheerleader. This requires the coach to distance himself from some aspects of the players' actions, including the specifics of some of their play. Knowing what the correct moves and plays are doesn't help at all, since **the coach can't play the game.** The actions of the players can sometimes take their minds for a ride, thus risking their concentration and focus. If a player begins to "lose his head" during a game, it is up to the coach to maintain a level of calm so that the game plan can again be the focus. To this end, it's crucial that **coaches must stay in control during the game.**

CHAPTER 12

A Team Must Play With Discipline

DISCIPLINE YOURSELF and others won't need to.

— JOHN WOODEN
FORMER UCLA BASKETBALL COACH

THE COACH'S LESSON

My boys had a hell of a time becoming disciplined. Many of them weren't very disciplined to begin with, and as a team they were often out of control. Early on, I was amazed at how quick the Rockies were to fight with the other team. It didn't take more than a bit of name-calling, or a strong bodycheck to get them mentally off of their game.

Many boys in their mid-teens deal with hostile emotions and find no other way to handle them except to lash out in anger. Unfortunately for these guys, they too often were trying to deal with uncalled for, and sometimes racially motivated, taunts from the other team. So as coaches, we found ourselves working as hard on helping our players develop self-control as we did on their offensive skills. Realizing what the boys had to cope with day in and day out, it was even more important to teach them how to deal with it all.

A lack of discipline need not manifest itself in physical or violent actions. More often, it can be as simple as a momentary mental lapse. While allowing that we're all human beings, prone to make mistakes, I pointed them out as often as was beneficial. The times when a player made a bone-headed play because of bad judgment were used to set examples of what not to do. I would spend an inordinate amount of time rehashing the play with the entire team. I'd try to speak to what the player was thinking or doing prior to making the mistake and then, in a painfully lengthy process, detail out the results. I did this not to be malicious, but to help all of us look at and evaluate our errors or misjudgments. I approached these discussions openly, saying, "If we don't talk about our own mistakes, we can't learn from each other."

There were also times when the lack of discipline proved to be too much. I had one player who was arguably one of our best. He was a big guy with a bruising style of play, and understanding his problems in life, I tolerated some of his angry outbursts on the ice. After all, the spirit of competition was alive and well in him. There were a number of times, however, when he crossed the line and selfishly vented too much of his own emotion and hurt the team. Each time, I had to discipline him. One time after completely losing his composure on the ice, the referee kicked him out of the game. At that point, he lost it and began swearing, threatening, and eventually charged towards the referee. The game was called off, and we forfeited the win.

Sure, there will be moments when we will make mistakes. But when poor judgment and loss of control become chronic, that indicates an obvious need for behavior change. It cannot be allowed to persist or the team's overall focus will be in jeopardy. That was the reason I kicked our best defenseman off of the team.

My decision surprised myself, as well as the others. It was not an easy call to make. Unfortunately, it had to happen. My hope was that I had taught the team that no lack of discipline or self-control could be allowed to hurt the team.

Winning Teams Play With Control

How often have you heard coaches lash out at players for incurring "stupid penalties" out of retaliation? Or players chastising other players for missing assignments? Infielders might complain about outfielders not charging "bloop" singles. A quarterback gets sacked because a fullback didn't pick up the block. Or it could be as obvious as a player arguing with an official out of frustration over a call. It happens all the time, and it's a lack of discipline that creates these situations.

No matter what the sport, the winning teams play with discipline. Every player has to keep his mind focused on the overall purpose of the team. A team prepares far too long to allow the game plan to be ruined by a momentary lack of judgment. Players must refuse to lose their cool, become selfish, or forget their tasks. A disciplined player must sacrifice his own personal emotional or egotistical needs for those of the team. It's much easier to execute a game plan when it is not subordinated to a player's loss of judgment.

The amount of detail that is included in the game plan is necessary for players to understand what and how they should perform. This detail helps players avoid or limit mistakes and assists them, as much as possible, in making real-time decisions based on pre-established criteria. Too much planning went into the overall strategy to allow the plan to be ignored. Players must stick to their assignments and their roles. That requires the kind of control that is rooted in self-discipline.

Disciplined Behavior in Practice and in Public

Discipline, of course, applies to more than just the game situation. Players must practice with the same work ethic and intensity. A team needs players to approach practice with a certain degree of professionalism. They also need to take seriously the opportunity that practices give them to improve their own game. This could also involve running laps on the field, shagging extra fly balls, or working out in the weight room afterwards. A well-disciplined team practices like it plays, and vice versa.

Of course, it doesn't stop on the playing surface, either. Players must exercise discretion and good judgment off of the field. Something seemingly personal, such as physical weight, can become a team issue. Behavior in public should be minded as well. It is too easy for a player to do something foolish that can create a distraction for his teammates. The Dallas Cowboys of the mid- to late '90s can attest to that. Instead of being asked about their preparations for their next opponent, Cowboys players constantly faced media questions about their coach being caught with a gun at an airport or their wide receiver being charged with assault.

Lesson from a Legend: Lou Holtz

 During Lou Holtz's tenure at both the University of Arkansas and Notre Dame, he was known as a straightforward disciplinarian. He drilled a high level of discipline into his players' behavior, their actions both on and off the field, and their mental state of preparedness. Holtz held tightly to the belief that if a team was regimented in its approach to a game then it would have better chances to perform in a disciplined manner during the game as well. As a result, Holtz's teams had tremendous success in situations where a lack of discipline can crush a team, such as trailing a favored team in a Bowl game. Coach Holtz set behavioral standards for his players, both on and off the field. He and his coaching staff outlined for the players the personal conduct requirements for all players. On the field was no different. Players were required to practice such simple acts as standing in a huddle. Holtz required players on the field to align their feet in the huddle and to all stand in the same, hands-on-their-knees position.

In a clear example of how this discipline manifests itself into good play during games, one need only look to the discipline of Holtz's offensive linemen before the snap of the ball. During Notre Dame practices, Holtz required his offensive linemen to practice how they assumed the set position. The linemen, after they left the huddle and approached the line of scrimmage, would all assume a position, wait for the quarterback to yell "Set, hit," and then they would all clap in unison before dropping to their three-point stance. Holtz drilled them in practices so that they would not only move in unison, but clap in unison, too. Holtz knew that if his players clapped together, they were in synch.

In his book *Winning Every Day*, Holtz affirms his belief in discipline and the basics, "When you have to pay attention to how you enter and break from a huddle, how you line up, and other seemingly minor details, it carries over when you execute larger assignments." During his years with the Irish, Holtz's offensive line rarely was called for offside penalties.

The Coach as Manager: Create a Well-Disciplined Work Group

In any organization, there are plenty of distractions for employees, as well as incidents that charge us with emotions. These occasions, if met without discipline, can result in poor judgment and mistakes. Like a sports team, the organization will suffer if one employee does not complete his or her task completely, correctly, or in a timely manner.

Think of how often a fellow employee has not finished her portion of an assignment. Or how a subordinate who does not carry out his direction according to plan jeopardizes the progress of the entire group while they wait for him to do it right. The reason for this infraction may be simple laziness, but it could also be a loose and unstructured atmosphere in preparation that later manifests itself as sloppy work on the job.

To reduce these problems, the manager must strive to create a well-disciplined work group that remains focused on the overall game plan. It cannot be stressed enough that all employee actions must support the overall goals, or they will be wasteful and destructive to varying degrees. The Japanese I met during a joint business venture would say, "If you're not adding quality to the product, then you're adding cost." That's a statement that absolutely demands discipline and adherence to the game plan.

To keep a group focused on the game plan during execution, they must understand all that has to be achieved. The important details of individual assignments must be highlighted. The interrelationships between employees must be understood. Team members must know when, where, and how they can impact the success of others. Therefore, the performance of the basics cannot be underrated. Of course, the time to ingrain these details is during the preparation phase, not during the game. This level of comprehension can happen best in the calmer period before the time of execution.

Professional Performance Includes Personal Conduct

In business, the need for discipline within an organization extends beyond professional performance to include personal conduct. With companies being held accountable for the actions of employees, it is increasingly important to maintain some ethical and behavioral standards. This emphasis should not only encompass actions that are impacting the team's execution of the game plan, but also any actions that could be interpreted as a reflection on the organization itself.

Here again, any lack of discipline must be met head-on with complete intolerance. The rest of the group must see that their manager is protecting the goals of the group, as well as protecting them individually from the effects of someone else's mistakes. If a team believes that their manager is adamant about the preservation of the overall organization's purpose, they're far more likely to believe in their manager's desire to win. This will only serve to strengthen the team's doctrine that the game plan cannot be sacrificed by a lack of discipline.

PUTTING THE LESSON IN ACTION

A lack of discipline can submarine the best plans. Coaching is a great teacher of this lesson. I began to make a point of highlighting any lapse in judgment that served as an example of undisciplined work performance, especially when it was emotionally motivated. These were the times when the team needed to see the effect of a mistake.

Now nobody likes to have a public spectacle made over their mistakes. In the context of most organizations, that's all it is. Someone gets berated in front of everyone for doing something dumb. However, in a learning organization that is focused on a game plan with an intimate understanding of the roles, mistakes and indiscretions can be used to teach lessons to the group.

Sure, it isn't always nice to make examples of other people in front of their peers. But if it's discussed with the employee privately first, and then later with the group in an open, learning atmosphere, it can have the desired result. My approach was simple. After discussing it first with the employee and reaching an understanding, I then talked about the "act of learning." I stressed to the employee that the team could learn a lesson of great value from this episode. In broaching the notion of making it a public lesson, I would say, "Any lesson that's learned by one person has value to the team. It would be even more beneficial if the rest of the group could learn it as well." I would finish with, "Would it bother you if we talked about this with the group so that they might benefit from this knowledge, too?" Of course, if the employee refused, then it was an opportunity lost. However, on a number of occasions, the reprimanded employee even volunteered to make a presentation to the group. This approach always showed respect for the individual.

Occasions will come when the indiscretion is so grave that the individual must be dealt with more severely. Here again, it must be met swiftly and directly. I have had to discharge employees who were continuously hurting the overall work group with their undisciplined work styles. However, once the employee was gone, I would make a point of telling the team about the infractions, mistakes, or behavior so they would understand that such lack of discipline would not be allowed to affect the team. More often than a manager likes to believe, the entire team usually knows about the discipline problem and is usually not surprised when the hammer falls on the perpetrator.

There was one particular incident that involved a subordinate who happened to be one of my friends outside of work. I had just taken over control of the department in which he worked. It became apparent that he was taking certain liberties and relaxing his attention to the game plan. Since he was always known for his excellent work, I assumed that this was a result of the comfort that comes with being the boss's buddy. I, however, had always kept a clear distinction between work and personal lives. I eventually found myself taking note of one too many of his inattentive mistakes. Assignments would be late or missed. Tasks were forgotten. Communication wasn't taking place with others.

I recall his look of disbelief when I explained to him why I had summoned him to my office. I found myself using the same words with him that I had used earlier in the locker room with my players. I explained to him that in the workplace, even *he* was not more important than the team. I explained how his lack of disciplined work was hurting the group, and why I would not tolerate those actions. I engaged him in a discussion, asking him to help identify the team members whom he had negatively impacted and how. Our discussion centered on the interrelationships with other team members that he had taken for granted. While the reprimand was only in the form of a warning, it was still a humbling moment for him.

It was crucial to maintain the discipline and commitment of the rest of the team during this time. Since the remainder of the department's leadership team knew of our outside friendship, I knew I had to address what others may have noticed already. My buddy had allowed our friendship to lull him into a false sense of security which, in turn, lowered his intensity and concentration. True to his professionalism, he quickly made a point of committing himself to his role with an added intensity after apologizing to his teammates for his miscues. The team, reciprocating that professional-ism, moved forward as if the matter had been resolved for good.

CHAPTER 13

The Coach Can't Play the Game

I DON'T BELIEVE A MANAGER EVER WON A PENNANT.

MY IDEA OF MANAGING is giving the ball to Tom Seaver and sitting down and watching him work.

— GEORGE "SPARKY" ANDERSON
FORMER MAJOR LEAGUE BASEBALL MANAGER,
CINCINNATI REDS, DETROIT TIGERS

THE COACH'S LESSON

I have always played hockey. All my life. That's what Canadians do. During my time coaching the Rockies, I was still actively playing in a competitive, adult men's hockey league. You can imagine the struggle in my mind between "Coach Rob" and "Rob the player." My problem was that I could never seem to turn off the player in me.

I often found myself trying to get into too much detail with players at the wrong time. I was always mentally playing every one of their shifts. I would be hollering orders like, "Cut to the left" or "There he is; pass it to him!" I would grab players as soon as they got to the bench to tell them what they should have done: "Hey, you had Damien coming across the blue line; if you made a move to the left of that man, you could have completed that pass." Let there be no mistake, my advice was futile more often than not.

In my early days of coaching, I tried talking to players on the bench after they came off of the ice. I would constantly lean over and try to teach. And oh, would I try! I would draw out movements and plays in front of their faces. My fingers would try to redirect their focus from the current action to spots on the ice that were meaningful minutes ago.

After a while, I couldn't help but notice their eyes. They were fixed on the game with an intense "I gotta get back in there" gaze. Or they would stare at me with a searching gaze, trying to recollect the moment I was talking about. (Since the game is moving so fast for them out there, they might have had a hard time recalling the detail that I was talking about.) They looked around me, beyond me, deaf and blind to everything I said and did. And for a moment I would be furious that they weren't listening to me. Then I'd remember my own playing days. Hell, I wasn't listening either.

Upon realizing this, I noticed my behavior and how ineffective it was. What I thought were valid pointers at the time were actually irrelevant for that particular player at that moment. I wasn't teaching them; instead, I was trying to play the game for them. I was momentarily taking the player's attention away from the game while I questioned something that had already happened. No matter how I looked at it, "task interference" and "micromanagement" were all that came to mind.

Obviously, I had to back off of my overbearing attempts to capture their minds with my lessons. I came to grips with the fact that I was ineffective as a teacher during the game, and I reevaluated my role. Knowing that my role was more important in the preparation and practice phase, I had to find ways to take advantage of that.

I forced myself to change my behavior on the bench. I stopped making a big deal out of little errors at the time. I quit trying to give pointers during the game to players who weren't paying attention. To put it mildly, I shut up. Any observations I made were used to build my training plans and my practice exercises. I refrained from making any statement regarding a player's moves, unless it was linked to our overall game strategy. Instead, I substituted a quick reminder of the overall game plan whispered in the ear of a player, or I said nothing. Somewhere along the way, I began to act like a coach—instead of a player.

While on the bench during a game, I began to make a habit of noting mistakes that were made on the ice. While done initially as a way to preoccupy myself, it helped me to maintain an analytical view of what was happening. I would pull out these notes during the next practice. We would review them and discuss what happened. Botched plays would manifest themselves in practice drills for playing units, or perhaps in individual lessons held away from the group. While I had to fight the urge to correct mistakes at game time, I found that waiting to do it during practice or in team meetings was much more advantageous. This allowed the team a better chance to grasp the lesson and to improve much more significantly upon their past performance.

After games, losses especially, there would be plenty of discussion from the group. Mistakes made by the team during game time were suddenly a little more tolerable if we could learn from them. We would use the next available opportunity to talk about our miscues, work on correcting them, and practice the skills to deal with similar situations again. This strategy allowed us to change our behavior by letting mistakes happen during games and waiting for a better opportunity to learn from them: practice.

The Coach as an Active Observer

A coach is responsible for developing the team. Training them. Teaching them to overcome their shortcomings. Leading them through adversity. He should nurture each player's individual role and develop different aspects of the player's game to help him become a more formidable foe. The coach must teach players how to win by delivering to them a game plan and preparing them to execute it. This is one of his major roles, but it's not one that he can play during the game.

At game time, the coach's role changes. Instead of being a teacher and mentor, the coach must learn to become an active observer. A coach must stand back and hope that the players execute the game plan that was created, discussed, and practiced. Oh sure, he can make adjustments to lines, change pitchers, or call different plays, but he is still a hostage to the players' ability to execute the game plan. That isn't an easy role to accept for many coaches.

It is one of the first and most difficult lessons for an ex-player turned coach to learn: The coach does not play the game. And no matter how much a coach may *want* to, he *can't* play it. Good coaches will understand the vital importance of staying in their prescribed role. A coach getting too involved in the details of the player's performance during a game can become counterproductive. Our impulse is to correct mistakes right then and there. We want to point it out to the player immediately. We *know* what the player should have done. Sure, we're coaches now, but most of us were players once upon a time. We know what the right plays are. Unfortunately, we're not the ones playing.

That can create a feeling of helplessness that will overcome any coach at some point while walking the bench. You're watching mistakes being made. Players are not following the game plan or adhering to their assignments. A player misses an open-field tackle that ends up in the end zone. The left fielder misjudges a line drive that drops for a triple. As much as he may want to, a coach really can't help that during a game. Nor should he try to.

Don't Try to Teach During the Game

A coach can't teach during a game. It's that simple. The fact is, it's hard enough to even get a player's attention during a game. Players who are gasping for oxygen and swimming in sweat and adrenaline are not listening intently to anything a coach says. The player is immersed in the game. Totally overcome with energy, emotion, fatigue. He sits on the bench and mentally rewinds through past plays. He watches the opponent's moves, looking to pick up something. He talks to himself. Chastises himself for poor mistakes or miscues. Urges himself to try harder. Tells himself to remember to do it differently next time. Talks to the teammate next to him about the blown play. A coach simply can't compete with that.

How can a coach expect any player to have reacted the same way he would have? The answer is, he can't. A coach trying to explain how he "would have done it" is only an attempt to clone the coach. Every one of us is different. We each have our own physical, mental, and emotional idiosyncrasies, and we may each react differently when presented with the same situation. Now, to each personality, add the speed of the game, factor in the surging adrenaline, and throw in a healthy dash of emotions, and you'll end up with wildly different reactions from everyone. That's why the coach has to accept that it's the *players* who must play the game.

Reinforce the Game Plan With Constructive Correction

Now keep in mind that a coach should reinforce the game plan. Correcting a player's positional play, strategical error, or failure to execute the game plan can help during a game. That's constructively moving the player towards the coach's vision of the overall team and its game plan. "Hey, remember we said all week that we have to bump that receiver as soon as he leaves the line of scrimmage. You need to get closer to him and contact him as soon as he jumps," would be an example of this type of correction in a football game. That kind of coaching needs to happen during a game so that the player's contribution is always focused. Correcting a player's situational responses can only help to support the team's game plan for that game.

There are plenty of lessons to be learned during a game, but they will not be lessons taught by the coach. Instead, they will be taught by the opponent, the referees, the environment, or any other outside influences. But what can that knowledge contribute during the game? Nothing. Those lessons refer to one-time events that may never happen again in that game, or another one. There is no need to correct it then and there. That may only serve to drag the player back to a moment in time in which he made a mistake, instead of staying focused on the overall game plan. Those lessons are best saved for later.

Lesson from a Legend: Scotty Bowman

For more than three decades, as the NHL's premiere coach, Scotty Bowman has built a solid reputation on his ability to prepare his teams to play consistently at championship caliber. During a career that has resulted in eight Stanley Cup championships, he has been known as a strict disciplinarian, a detailed strategist, and the league's preeminent tactician. Despite his success and his stature, Bowman hasn't always been liked by his players. In fact, many are on record as saying they hated playing for him, although they respected him for his knowledge, his preparation, and his ability to put together and teach a game plan. This speaks more to his strong-handed approach to practicing, following team rules, and simply giving one's best effort during every game, than it does to him as a person.

Despite Bowman's attention to the details of teaching, he is best known for his role during game time. In what seems like a complete change in purpose, Bowman lets go of all teaching and simply deals with matching up player lines with those of the opponent. In hockey, this practice is known as "running the bench." And Scotty Bowman is the best in the business.

In hockey, teams normally play a game with three or four lines, consisting of a center and two wingers. These lines normally will cycle through in order, except for adjustments to match up with the lines of opposing teams. For example, if a coach is "running the bench" he might make certain that his best defensive checking line is on the ice at the same time the opposing team's most potent offensive line is.

Bowman focuses solely on this task, one that was first mastered by a predecessor of his in Montreal, Dick Irvin. Requiring great patience by a coach, this task may only lead to perhaps a few mismatches during a game. However, that may be all a team needs: to have their best line on the ice, while the opposing team's best are catching their breath sitting on the bench. Showing the understanding of all the team's necessary roles, Bowman puts just as much effort into matching up his defensive players with the enemy's best scorers. Speaking of Bowman's work from behind the bench, former NHL coach and general manager Al MacNeil said, "Scotty perfected it. He's a line or two ahead of whoever he's coaching against."

Throughout his coaching career, Bowman's players have noticed that he serves a purpose behind the bench during games. While noting positive and negative observations for future feedback, Bowman also contributes in the only other way he can by manipulating player match-ups. His players recognize that. Former coach, player, and general manager Cliff Fletcher has said that Bowman's players "knew they only had to be as good as the other team. Scotty would make the difference."

The Coach as Manager: Preparation Is Your Top Priority

All of the team's preparation is practice for the moments when each individual employee must perform his or her role to execute the plan and help achieve the organization's goal. That is "game time." During these situations, the quality of execution will almost always be directly proportionate to the quality of the preparation. Because of this, a manager should always be less concerned with the event itself and more focused on laying the groundwork and shaping the group to meet the challenges of the event.

Employees, while engaged in the performance of their role, will and must be focused on their duties. They must be attuned to the immediate and dynamic challenges presented by their customers, their tasks, or their workforce. Intensity must be focused on the task. And chances are, it will be. If they have been prepared, they will carry out their actions like players who have practiced the same moves every day for weeks.

Because the period of preparation is more crucial for managers than the actual moment of execution, the development and preparation of employees is one of the manager's biggest challenges. That is a tough thought to accept, especially if you're a manager who likes to get involved with the day-to-day activities of your work group. The fact is that a manager is much more useful to employees as a teacher, guide, and coach during preparation, then as an assistant, or worse yet, an interruption, during the completion of work.

Delegate, Delegate, Delegate

In business, it's not always easy for any boss to "let go" of tasks and trust employees to perform them well. It is, however, necessary. A manager must delegate tasks to employees and allow them to perform those duties. It's unrealistic to think that any good manager can be involved in every detail. Unfortunately, some managers believe they can.

In most workplaces, managers were once something other than the manager. Chances are they once did similar work at similar levels as the people who report to them. More often than not, they have risen through the ranks from the grunt jobs to the upper echelon. Rarely does a manager arrive on the scene without historical references to, or experience in, the work that is being performed.

While this experience can help managers be great teachers and coaches, it can also set the scene for "micromanagement," a common problem cited by many workers as a prime reason for lack of productivity. It frustrates, distracts, and often confuses employees, and it is seldom confined to the lower ranks of organizations, either. It has more to do with a manager's need to become involved in the details of a job than the employee.

A manager who has a different idea about how a task should be performed will often express it. It may be in the form of direction for a future task, or criticism of a past action. The problem comes when the manager questions an individual's actions while it is happening—for example, the manager who points out a customer service rep's mistakes while the rep is taking calls from customers. Now, here again, a correction of an employee's actions as they align to the overall direction of the work group is one thing. That would be acceptable and in line with a manager's role to keep everyone focused on the same overall objective while executing a common plan. However, a deep dive into the "how to's" is unlikely to be constructive at a time when the action is still happening.

Since managers have the ability to impact their subordinates' livelihoods, any direction that managers provide will have an effect. Often the result is some form of a knee-jerk reaction in an attempt to appease "the boss." An employee may totally change what he or she is working on, or how, as a result of the boss's direction. The end result is still the same: it's a distraction. If a manager seeks to intervene at any time, it will be an interruption to the employee, regardless of what the intervention was for. It absolutely *will* take the employee's attention away from the task at hand, but the manager still will not have the employee's full attention to learn at that moment.

PUTTING THE LESSON IN ACTION

Every workday, I see managers and leaders questioning employees' actions or the details of their work. You probably see it in your organization, too. Just sit through a presentation and watch as managers question the way data is being summarized or how statements are worded, and you'll see it. It's a hard habit to break. I still do it myself on occasion, although not as frequently as I used to.

I remember catching myself once. I was reviewing a package of material that an employee had prepared for distribution. It was an interpretation of data that led to a number of conclusions, and she had worked for several days preparing it. We needed this information quickly in order to make some crucial decisions.

As I was reading, I reached for a red pen. I began to scribble on the pages, "Change this font." "Bold here." "This page looks too busy." Soon, I had created the blueprint for completely rewriting the report. I had successfully given this employee specific instructions on how to make this report look like one that I would have written.

As I handed it back, I saw the look of frustration, disgust, and futility in the face of my assistant. She assured me that it would be no trouble to make the changes and that she would be happy to rework it. With that she left, with three days' worth of wasted work under her arm. It took me a couple of minutes to realize what I had done.

Then the coach in me stepped in. "Step back from the game! Stand behind the players' bench!" I told myself. I had to change my mentality. I could be more useful to the group if I stepped back from the action and looked for opportunities to teach, develop, and help. I would have to step back far enough so that I could not interfere, but close enough to watch and critique my employees' performance. I had to be a coach.

I chased after her, brought her back into the office, and took back the marked-up copy. Reviewing it, I ignored everything that had previously caught my superficial disapproval and focused on content. I read it over and quickly grasped that her interpretation was on target and would definitely point us in the correct direction. I only made a few recommendations. These I wrote on a separate piece of paper and handed that to her as my edits. I kept the marked-up package for my own waste bin. Needless to say, she left my office with a different attitude.

CHAPTER 14

Coaches Must Stay in Control During the Game

---

*ONE REASON I SO SELDOM REACTED to a big
Cowboys' play was because I hardly ever saw any of
our offensive plays. I always knew what play we
had called. I didn't have to watch it. The only
uncertainty was how the opposition reacted; it was
their defense I needed to watch and analyze so I
would know best how to counter it.*

— TOM LANDRY
FORMER NFL COACH, DALLAS COWBOYS

THE COACH'S LESSON

For the Detroit Rockies, discipline was a regular element of our overall
style. The assistant coaches and I preached discipline every chance we could
get, whether in preparations or during games. We always envisioned our

THE BUSINESS OF WINNING

players being able to methodically work their way through any situation, oblivious to any distraction, verbal or otherwise. So we constantly worked to change any negative behavior, rule violations, or emotional "meltdowns." Unfortunately, it wasn't always that way. And it was never easy. Not even for me as a coach.

I remember one game where I was convinced that our hockey team was on the receiving end of a referee's personal prejudices. I was becoming furious as our players continued to end up on the wrong side of his calls. Now, we had always taught the kids to rise above that kind of adversity. They had become disciplined (and thick-skinned) by then. That evening, however, it was I who lost it. My blood had boiled for too long. At one point, I unleashed a tirade against the ref that ended with me throwing some sticks onto the ice. The referee correctly threw my misbehaving butt out of the game.

What I remember to this day, oddly enough, isn't how I felt or what I did. It's the expressions on our players' faces, and what they said as I walked off the bench. They looked at me with both surprise and disappointment. Their normally cool, level-headed coach had self-destructed in rage. Everyone fell silent on the bench as they watched me. Then one turned back to the ice, and said to a teammate, "Well, what do we do now?" The boy next to him replied, "We lose, that's what."

I've often reflected on that moment. While I had forgotten what my role was during the game, my players hadn't. It's important for a coach to remain the steady, dependable source of guidance and inspiration for a team. Nothing should be allowed to affect that, especially a selfish act of uncontrolled emotion. That event sensitized me to the effect of these types of occurrences. Whenever one of my players had a similar "meltdown," I noticed how distracting it was to the other players. That kind of behavior cost us mentally—not only the player involved, but perhaps even some of his teammates.

Good Coaches Keep Their Emotions in Check

Game time is an emotional time for players. Some throw up before a game. Some are so superstitious as to eat the same meal before any game. To a player, the game is an adrenaline-packed, super-charged, soul-sweating reason to exist. At game time, the calmest of men can become the angriest, nastiest, most foul-mouthed human being on the planet. A coach, however, must be different.

It is up to the coach to remain unruffled by what is transpiring on the playing field. While high and low emotions are carrying players deeper and deeper into the game, the coach must remain above that. He must avoid becoming emotionally involved. True, no coach can ever totally remove his feelings from the game; however, they must be removed as much as possible from any decision making.

Remember: players want to believe that the coach has a plan, even when they think all is lost. Desperate players will look to the coach for any hint that his plan can still work, if executed properly. If a coach loses control of himself and begins to rant and rave, players may lose faith in their ability to overcome their opponent. How can they believe in the coach's plan and its chances of success? The coach has to maintain the intense focus on the game plan, and do it with some degree of tranquility.

Lesson from a Legend: John Wooden

 The UCLA Bruins didn't win twelve national titles in a row without playing a disciplined game. The truth is that Coach John Wooden built a legacy of teams that prepared, practiced, and played with strict discipline. And so, the Bruins were known for their professional, businesslike approach to doing their "job." Often, writers and commentators would remark at what seemed like a complete lack of emotion on the faces of Bruin players, even after incredible plays or emotional comebacks.

Acting as the only example the young Bruins would need, Coach Wooden was the model of game-time discipline. He was sure to remain calm and composed throughout any situation. Rarely allowing emotional outbursts to get the better of him, he remained in control. To Wooden, in order for him to be at the top of his own "game" as a coach, he needed to stay focused on his own tasks.

Wooden's Bruins were taught to focus solely on their preparation and their own play. As former Bruin and NBA star Bill Walton later remarked to Charlie Jones, "Coach Wooden always taught us that it wasn't so much about competing against the opponent as it was about competing against an ideal, a level of perfection as opposed to just winning the game. Coach Wooden warned us so many times: 'Don't beat yourself.'"

Kareem Abdul Jabbar, another Wooden pupil, and, along with Walton, one of the few people to be in both the college and NBA Halls of Fame, took the same "coolness" to heart. Jabbar says, "Coach taught us self-discipline, and was always his own best example. He discouraged expressing emotion on the court, stressing that it would eventually leave you vulnerable to opponents."

The Coach as Manager: Maintain Your Objectivity

In our work environment, the boss is always the boss. Regardless of how friendly or chummy we may get, the person in the bigger office is usually the one who is obeyed. Whether there exists an open atmosphere or not, the boss will normally be the person who the subordinates will look to or come to for guidance.

Managers who become emotionally involved with any project, task, or undertaking will undoubtedly begin to lose some degree of objectivity. Decisions that normally would be attacked from a rational, non-partisan viewpoint may become somewhat one-sided. While that result may please employees who are fighting with vigor on the emotional front, it may not be in the best interests of the business.

Additionally, managers who begin to react more from the stomach and heart, and less from the business mind will risk losing the respect of both their subordinates and peers. Employees and peers don't want to think for a moment that the authoritative figures that they look to for guidance and support are "out of control." Managers who undermine their subordinates' belief in their decision-making abilities will suffer the ensuing loss of credibility. Additionally, the loss of confidence in the boss, as well as the boss's plan, can only make it more difficult for employees to carry out their assignments well.

Make no mistake about it, this is not easy. Often times, a manager naturally reacts to situations based on emotions. Anger is the most obvious. Unleashed rage might lead to permanent damage in the employee-manager relationship, or at the worst, premature dismissal of an employee. A manager's sense of personal ownership of a product may provoke him or her to defend that product in spite of discouraging data. A manager's personal preference for a certain region of the country might protect a deteriorating sales region from being eliminated.

What is often underestimated, however, is the employee's ability to see these emotionally tainted decisions for what they really are. If subordinates believe that a manager has arrived at the wrong conclusion based on personal emotions, their belief in the decision, the game plan, and the manager will begin to erode.

PUTTING THE LESSON IN ACTION

I can recall too many incidents in which my credibility as a sound, rational, consistent manager went out the window in my employees' eyes. Early in my career, I benefited from a series of quick promotions. I was constantly striving to overcome my young appearance with a mature, calm approach to issues. Thus I was always conscious of how I came across. Knowing that everyone was watching to see my reactions, I always tried to maintain my composure at all times. But all it would take is one lapse of control.

I remember one effort which occurred in the Maintenance organization in one of our plants. We had been encouraging the supervisors to plan their weekend projects in advance. If we could have these projects prepared at the beginning of the shifts on Saturdays, with parts and prints ready to go, then we might not have skilled tradesmen sitting, reading the paper for the first half hour, waiting to be assigned.

We began early in this effort, which involved preparation over the previous days, documentation of assignments, and contact with tradesmen prior to the weekend. Not all of the supervisors had used our new process yet. However, one morning, while walking through the area in a somewhat foul mood, I reacted to what I saw: people sitting, reading the newspaper, waiting to be assigned. I suspended six skilled tradesmen on the spot and sent them home indefinitely and immediately went searching for the supervisors.

When I found them, these supervisors looked at me with a mixture of surprise and frustration. True enough, the employees were not working, but the supervisors had not given them any assignments. Who was really responsible? It turned out that the reason the tradesmen had not been assigned at the time was that there was an emergency breakdown that had preoccupied the supervisors as they determined how best to dispatch the workers. Not only had I intervened into the activities of these supervisors, but also since my methods were contractually wrong, I ended up giving their employees a paid day off. Two projects had to be cancelled, since I had sent the maintenance tradesmen home. I could read the disgust on some of their faces, while a couple were bold enough to confirm it to my face.

Normally in this type of situation, I would have watched from a distance, made my summaries, and proceeded to either reprimand or reinforce behavior with the supervisors appropriately. This would have been used as anecdotal evidence that our plans to change how we assigned employees was the right way to go. An excellent example of what I had been preaching all along, it could have been an excellent teaching opportunity. Instead, it was a lesson in embarrassment for me.

This episode was a clear and extreme example of task interference, which resulted in employee anger and frustration, not to mention my subordinates looking at me as a reactionary and possibly incompetent manager. I still use this recollection to remind myself at times when I sense I'm getting too involved. It never hurts to constantly remind ourselves of the lessons we've learned, especially the ones you would rather not repeat.

How to Become a
Highly Effective Sideline Manager

➤ **Step 1: Recognize when it's game time.**
Game time refers to:

- ❏ Any time when you are **not** planning, preparing, teaching, or learning. Conversely, it is any time you are doing, implementing, or executing.

- ❏ An event, action, or activity that:

  ___ Can't be interrupted.

  ___ You have planned or prepared for.

  ___ Is either the executable action listed in the game plan or is crucial to the success of the game plan.

➤ **Step 2: Understand that your role as manager at game time is different from any other time.**
Here are some tips to help you become a highly effective sideline manager.

DON'T...

- ❏ Lose objectivity by getting emotionally involved in a project, task, or undertaking.

- ❏ Attempt to teach while employees are trying to execute. (Remember that the added pressure of game time performance can minimize the impact of your lessons on your team.)

- ❏ Try to correct mistakes. Save this for the next appropriate learning opportunity unless your employees are jeopardizing the game plan irreparably. In many cases (such as when practice or lengthy discussions are required), it would be ineffective to attempt to correct mistakes during game time.

- ❏ Otherwise interrupt the execution of the plan.

- ❏ Be an unnecessary distraction.

- ❏ Make corrections based primarily on "how I would've done it."

DO...

❑ Analyze the actions of your staff and your team's progress toward the overall objective (save your analysis and share it with your team only when the action has subsided).

❑ Make necessary adjustments and corrections to keep your team aligned, but do so unobtrusively and only when you know that you can make an impact.

❑ Be available as a resource.

❑ Be a source of guidance, advice, and motivation.

❑ Reinforce the game plan whenever possible.

❑ Reinforce positive observations whenever possible.

❑ Keep an eye on your identified opponents.

❑ Plan the next "down time" learning opportunity.

❑ Assess the support structure that you've developed (what's working and what's not working as expected).

❑ Look for ways to remove obstacles for employees.

❑ Maintain discipline and adherence to the game plan by unobtrusively maintaining the team's focus on the game plan and reemphasizing unit responsibilities and individual assignments.

❑ Step in when an employee has lost emotional control or is otherwise acting contrary to the team playing style in a way that is compromising the execution of the game plan.

The Business of Winning

Section 4

Learn from the Game After the Game

IT'S WHAT YOU LEARN after you know it all that counts.

— JOHN WOODEN
FORMER UCLA BASKETBALL COACH

There is nothing more definitive in sports than a game. A team either wins or fails to win. The outcome passes verdict on the game plan, the players' preparation, and the team's execution. Nothing can change the outcome. However, you can control a team's reaction to the results of a game. This holds true for any team that has to execute a plan— sports or business.

As part of a sports team's continuous cycle of learning, practicing, and executing, the game serves an important purpose. If studied and assessed properly, it can be a useful resource—offering countless opportunities to reinforce previous lessons learned or to generate new ones. After studying games, a coach may alter the direction of the game plan, the practices, and the players' roles. Win or lose, there are gains to be made that will benefit the team's continuous development.

These same learning opportunities exist in business, as the team members execute their roles on a regular basis. Every day will bring instances when employees will be in a position to act or respond in a manner that will support the overall team plan. Since these "games" happen more often in business than in sports, the manager must be prepared to reinforce the team members' performance more often than a sports coach.

The benefit of any observations and lessons from games will be optimized if they are discussed, accepted, and comprehended by the entire team. Better yet, if the whole team can make the observations together, using game films, for example, then this assessment process is even more meaningful. Regardless, it will be up to the manager to ensure that each performance serves a purpose, which will underscore the team's future preparation.

Obviously, failure can help a team's development, since many lessons originate from failure. For that reason, managers are quick to utilize an unsuccessful effort to reinforce game plans. Maybe too quick, sometimes. To a manager who is strictly focused on the end result, it may seem implausible that there would be any reason for celebration outside of complete and total success.

These managers and their teams then miss the opportunities to learn from success, to feel good about their progress, and to reinforce their shared work. (Remember, team members need to believe in the game plan.) Too many managers fail to pause for—or even acknowledge the value of—small celebrations, which are excellent tools for reinforcing the game plan and the team's effort.

Games provide the opportunity to reinforce the behavior of team members, good or bad. While mistakes and poor judgment can be tolerated to some degree in practice, they hurt a team in games. Additionally, the entire team is watching during a game. This creates a difficult position for the manager to be in, as he or she may have to react to a team member's conduct. In the workplace, with laws, ethical standards, and fair treatment policies to guide us, it is even more critical for the manager to maintain high behavior standards. Also, a momentary lapse in judgment can have a significant impact on the team's overall goals. Personal conduct guidelines, team rules, and adherence to the plan must all be reinforced by the manager.

Most important to this phase in the development of a team is the reinforcement of the game plan. After performances, all team members' actions, responses, behaviors, judgments, etc. must be measured against the game plan. In the period of reflection after a game, there will be a limited amount of time to attach the results to the team's preparation. And that's the time for a manager to return to the role of teacher.

As the learning cycle of a team returns the team members back to the game plan, they must use everything gained from a game, good or bad. The notion that the whole is greater than the sum of the parts must be an over-riding principle for the team, so much so, that **no single player will ever be more important than the team.** To the manager, it is essential to use the games as reinforcement of good performance. A team should always take time out to **celebrate little victories.** Positive behavior should be rewarded positively. If there is a need to react to improper conduct, then performances should initiate that review, as well. With all eyes of the team on him or her, the manager must respond fairly and consistently to team members who have acted inappropriately. The manager should strive to **treat players equally.** Whether positive or negative, equal treatment reinforces the team's unity. Finally, it's important that each team member **always remember why you won or lost.** Much can be gained from the game experience; don't miss the opportunity to learn from the game—after the game.

CHAPTER 15

No Single Player Will Ever Be More Important Than the Team

My responsibility is to get twenty-five guys playing for the name on the front of their uniform and not for the one on the back.

— Tommy Lasorda
FORMER BASEBALL MANAGER, Los Angeles Dodgers

THE COACH'S LESSON

We had a few guys on the Rockies team that were head and shoulders above the rest. They reveled in that fact. They loved to score goals. At times, they seemed to exude arrogance. Being adolescents with competitive spirits and dreams of their own, the others responded by trying to score goals, too. This reaction tended to manifest itself in a lack of passing and an over-enthusiastic display of one-man scoring attempts.

Realizing that I had to keep the team in an unselfish frame of mind, I made attempts to equalize where I could. In practices, I frequently stopped plays when any one player made a selfish move. While reviewing films, I highlighted the excellent passes made by marginal players. In the dressing room after games, I recognized the players who received assists on goals, and made little mention of the goal scorers. I criticized one-man scoring attempts that were selfish, even if they resulted in a goal. I discouraged players from talking or bragging about statistics in the dressing room. I tried to do anything I could to make the cocky ones humble, and the humble ones proud.

It was not long before the players began to quote me, "No single player will ever be more important than the team." It became a favorite anthem of mine. I applied it to all responsibilities of the players. I associated it to any discipline that was handed out. I used it to explain why I rotated goalies every game. It became a prevalent guideline for everything we did.

When I look back at the team that finally grew and eventually won, I can see that it was one homogenous group of guys. There were no superstars among them, despite the statistics that suggested otherwise. There were no guys that were too small to contribute, regardless of physical dimensions. No one playing line was more important than any other, even though their playing time might have differed. In its simplest form, they were a team.

The Same Purpose, the Same Style, the Same Resolve

As discussed previously, it's important for a team to play within their pre-scribed roles. Once they have developed the ability to play in this context with control and discipline, they are ready to move to the next level: becoming part of the whole where the sum is greater than the parts. A team has to act like a team. It has to think, grow, react, learn, and feel like a team. There can be nothing in their collective minds more important than the team's success. They must move mentally and physically with the same purpose, the same style, and the same resolve. Only then can a coach lead and direct one true entity.

This group of individuals has to be so totally focused on the goals of the entire group that they subordinate their personal goals. Players must allow the needs of the team to supercede their own. That's a humbling step for anyone to take. It requires selflessness, trust, and a desire to win. A player's total commitment to the team encourages others to do the same. As a natural result, a stronger bond develops among a group of people who realize that they will do anything to help each other win. That's the kind of spirit that makes a championship team. From a coach's standpoint, this is the only acceptable behavior for the players. No one single player can be allowed to think that he is more important than the team—or more important than any other player. This attitude will only divide the team.

Of course, if coaching experience has taught us anything, it's that it's not totally up to the players. If the coach has prepared a sound game plan and focused the team on it, developed his players and their roles, and reinforced the lessons learned during the execution of the game plan, then the players can truly become united. The game plan unites the individuals and forges them into a team. California psychotherapist Dr. Lew Richfield is a leading "teammender;" he specializes in team building within corporations and mergers. He states, "Teams break when they don't have a goal or the goals aren't clearly defined by the leaders. Goals have to be firmly entrenched, otherwise people begin to operate as independent entrepreneurs in a system that really needs cooperative work."

We see this frequently in professional sports. The media regularly hypes up one star player while seemingly ignoring his fellow players on the team. The leading scorer gets a huge contract that dwarfs those of his teammates. On an ongoing basis, the coach is faced with obstacles in his attempt to create a team that is mentally and spiritually on the same level. These obstacles may even be external to the team. As the coach tries to keep the players' heads from swelling in the dressing room, reporters and commentators are pumping them up on the outside. Since most players read the newspapers and watch TV, the implied difference between players can become an obstacle.

Look at a championship team, however, and you normally don't see that. The Chicago Bulls of the '90s won championship after championship with the greatest basketball player of all times leading them. While everyone kept talking about Michael Jordan being the biggest reason the Bulls were so successful, Jordan himself disagreed with them. In countless interviews, Jordan denied any notion of the Bulls being a one-man team. He would often speak of the nights when he "didn't show up" and they still won. He reminded one reporter that there are always "five players on the court at any one time." Think of the impact that has on the guys that are sitting on the bench next to basketball greatness. Visualize the locker room where that kind of an attitude exists. That, of course, is a unified team. And in the end, it's a winning team.

Lesson from a Legend:
Tony DiCicco & The U.S. Women's National Soccer Team

There are so many great stories to come out of the decade-long success of the U.S. Women's National Soccer Team. They have made tremendous progress in establishing women's soccer as a viable, major sport. They have inspired spectators and generated fans where few existed before. Their enthusiasm for their sport, their team, and each other individually is addictive because it is completely pure and genuine.

The women's team won the World Cup in 1991 and was third in 1995; they also won a gold medal in the 1996 Olympics and the World Cup again in 1999. Throughout this period, they have been a team that resembles a family more than anything else. All fierce competitors, these women are united in their desire to be world champions. Nothing else will do.

On a team that boasts international stars who get mobbed by autograph seekers wherever they go, the players are decidedly low-key about any status. While Mia Hamm may have a building named after her at the NIKE world headquarters campus, she takes her regular turn unloading the equipment off of the team bus. Players such as Carla Overbeck, Michelle Akers, or Brandi Chastain all have endorsement deals as well, but they pull no special treatment from either coaches or their peers.

The coach of the U.S. Women's Soccer Team, Tony DiCicco, explains, "If you see the equipment list for practice, you'll see Hamm's name up there, Akers' name up there, (Julie) Foudy's name up there. We don't have a rookie responsible to handle those things, because we ought to do it together on the field and we ought to do it together off the field. And that's the way they want it."

That's the kind of team unity that manifests itself in success. Throughout the fifteen years that the team has been in existence, they have won just under 80 percent of their games.

The Coach as Manager:
Even the Boss Is a Member of the Team

When managing a group of people, managers must deal with many different emotions, egos, and personalities. People need attention. They want responsibility and all the trappings that come with it. And, of course, at the end of the pay period, they want to be rewarded for all that they've done. Since paychecks and egos are both personal items, this ensures the chance of clashes between the goals of the individual and those of the team.

Often we see an individual looking for better treatment or more attention than his or her teammates are getting. It may be the person's belief that diligent, hard work deserves it. Or it might just be the misperceptions of self-worth that an ego can create. It could be a selfish employee who, out of greed or misguided aspirations, is only looking out for himself or herself and couldn't care less about the rest. This person might be getting attention from people outside the group, or even from higher management, and this attention is going to his or her head. People like these exist in all organizations. They are the ones who believe that they are invaluable and serve a purpose that is greater than that of their peers.

Like in sports, this isolationist approach can only serve to break a team apart. The effect of selfish behavior is predictable: it minimizes the roles of the other individuals and trivializes their accomplishments. Since the success of one's career can have a significant impact on the quality of one's life, competition is not taken lightly by employees. They can therefore become incensed enough to react. And the infighting begins.

For the manager, any threat to the unity of the team must be met head on. Here again, no one employee can ever be more important than the company. A selfish individual and a focused, unified team will rarely share the same agenda. Employees who continue to care only about their personal goals will never take the team's well-being into consideration. Think of what Michael Miliken, the "Junk Bond King," did to his brokerage company. While he raked in hundreds of millions of dollars in bonuses year after year, he put his company at risk because of his illegal practices. Eventually, he was convicted and sent to prison, while his company, left almost bankrupt after legal settlements, was eventually purchased outright by another brokerage firm. It seems to be a natural and predictable phenomenon. When individuals are allowed to concentrate only on their own personal objectives and continue to be rewarded, then the organization suffers.

To build a true team, the manager has to egotistically ground some people, while emotionally elevating others. Those playing less glamorous roles on the team must be encouraged to feel worthwhile. Their work needs to get attention, too. While they may not be as good, nor grab as much attention as others, if a manager has truly utilized them in a role, then they too are contributing greatly. The stars of the team need to know, understand, and appreciate the work of the other players. They're the ones that need to realize that it takes more to making a group successful than just the achievements of a select few.

In turn, everyone on the team needs to understand and believe in the interdependence that unites them. They need to know the challenges that exist for each person. If they can appreciate the workload or challenges that others face, then respect and appreciation of fellow workers is not far behind. A true team can't exist without it.

This, of course, applies to the boss, as well. As part of the team, the manager cannot become more important than the overall group. His or her personal goals and aspirations can never enter into the daily work activities. Chances are good such goals and aspirations would be recognized for what they are: self-centered. When a group of subordinates sees that the manager is really only looking out for himself or herself, then what is their motivation to perform well? What do they perceive as the purpose of the team? Why should they pull together, other than to defend themselves against the boss? For this reason, managers must be mindful of their role as members of the team.

PUTTING THE LESSON IN ACTION

I tried to apply the same philosophies at work that I was using at the arena. I began to pay more attention to the people I had placed in basic positions. They were far from the limelight, performing work that was less glamorous than most. I appreciated their tasks and the difficulties they faced daily. Whenever I had the opportunity, I began to "educate" the rest of the team on the purpose, difficulty, and benefits of the work these grunts were doing. I went out of my way to publicly acknowledge accomplishments that directly supported the achievement of the team's goals. Reinforcing the overall objectives of the group, while at the same time highlighting the contributions of individuals, helped to bring some "big-headed folks" back to the same level as the rest.

The approach I took with my better employees was somewhat different. With them, I was ever watchful for any signs of "attention starvation." If they seemed to be seeking me out for petty reasons, or glaring when I was spending too much time with other employees, I would try to make contact with them. I made a point of outwardly appreciating their efforts by mentioning some specific task that they recently did well. Then I would balance this by noting someone else's accomplishment, such as, "Can you believe what Bob did? I thought there was no way he could get that data compiled by today. That sure helps you and me by giving us an extra day's worth of analysis before Tuesday's meeting." This would inevitably bring a matching acknowledgment from my star employee. I like to think that it made them realize some of the accomplishments that helped the team.

In our status-update meetings, I went out of my way to give everyone equal time to present their team's update to the entire group. These were delivered in the form of status reports. If someone didn't have an update to give, then I would always be sure to ask him or her about a project or assignment currently in progress. I would continue to ask questions, while others seemed disinterested. My theory was that the amount of time that I spent listening would lend some significance to the work. It also educated others on what their fellow team members were doing to contribute to the goals.

On occasion, I would have to deal with an employee who acted selfishly. If it impacted the team, or even just another team member, then the employee's behavior had to be addressed. One time, a particularly self-centered employee had strayed from a game plan to do something for my boss. In the meantime, he had let some of his assignments slip, causing our team to lose ground. When I finally confronted him, I spent a considerable amount of time explaining that my reasons for being upset had nothing to do with him "going over my head," but rather that for a moment, he turned his back on his team. Just to illustrate the point further, I invited my boss into the office to listen as I explained the negative impact on the work group. Hearing this, my boss then apologized to me. He explained to my subordinate that he would have never wanted the overall objectives of the team to suffer for any reason. Hearing the "Big Boss" explain that even *he* was not more important than the team sent a clear message to my subordinate.

CHAPTER 16

Celebrate Little Victories

WINNING IS NOT EVERYTHING—but making the effort to win is.

— VINCE LOMBARDI
FORMER NFL FOOTBALL COACH, GREEN BAY PACKERS

THE COACH'S LESSON

Sports is filled with emotions, and to expect players to keep them bottled up at a time when they are jubilant is unreasonable. Our team was no exception. After a goal, every player would jump up from the bench, screaming and high-fiving each other. Even I was pumping a fist in the air. Even if the goal only cut the other team's lead to two goals instead of three, it was still big for us.

With the Rockies, we were so desperate for victories in the very beginning that we couldn't help but celebrate. Since there was a certain degree of relief when we finally notched a win, I was tolerant of any wild antics from the boys. In the dressing room, they hollered about how each one of them was a star out there and boasted of who laid the best hit on the other team.

Just listening to them, you would have thought they had just won the Olympic gold medal.

After a victory with that level of emotion, a coach has to manage it properly. The players have to celebrate for a while. They *need* to celebrate. My only concern was that they kept their focus on the big picture. So I would step forward in the dressing room for a few words, but only a few. I would always be careful to frame any one victory in the context of our overall plight. While we had a long way to go, any victory was reinforcement that we were on the right track. As always, it was important to highlight what we had done well in that game and how it resulted from the execution of our overall plan. My words to them in the dressing room were always positive and encouraging. I wanted them to feel good not only about winning, but also about successfully executing the game plan we had worked on so much. After saying my piece, I found that the best thing for me to do was to step aside and let them high-five each other for a while.

A season where you only win 15 percent of your games is a long season. It's difficult to keep your heart in it at that rate. I had only to look at the faces of the parents after small victories to see even more reasons to allow for little celebrations. They sat in a cold arena game after game, watching some pretty ugly losses. Unfortunately for them, they didn't know our overall plan. They didn't hear the confidence with which we talked in the dressing room or at practice. So when a victory came along, they were as excited as any one of us.

Trying to keep fifteen teenaged boys from the inner-city of Detroit interested in playing hockey wasn't always easy. For that reason, it was important to keep them enthused. Letting them celebrate, strut, act cocky, or simply hoot and holler in the moments after a game was one way to let them go home feeling good. It was also sure to result in more enthusiasm at the next practice.

Victory Comes in Many Small Successful Steps

Sports teams fight for everything they get. "Blood, sweat, and tears" pour out on any game field or court. Athletes and coaches crave victory; that's why they exist. If a team is trained well and focused, then total victory is all it will accept.

But what happens when a baseball player hits a home run in the third inning? What does the team on the bench do when their running back crosses the goal line in the first quarter? What does a basketball team do after a three-point play? They jump up and down, hug each other, scream, holler, and act as if they just won the championship. But only for a moment. Then they sit back down and refocus on the job at hand, since the game is not yet won.

They know that the victory will only come after many small successful steps. It could take four touchdowns to beat an opposing football team. It might take three goals to win a soccer game. Players realize that the game cannot be won without these small achievements all adding up. That's why they celebrate them as little victories. They will high-five the home-run hitter and then, appropriately, settle back down after that jubilant moment because there is a "lot of baseball to play yet tonight."

And what does the coach do? Does he holler at his players to sit back down and quit celebrating because they haven't won anything yet? Does he chastise them if they end up celebrating prematurely for a home run, but end up losing the game in the end? Of course not. He allows, if not encourages, the team to celebrate the little victories.

A team needs to generate positive energy. They might need to revive their hopes of winning, or to reinforce the feeling that they are playing well. Individual players may need the emotional lift that only a joyous group hug can bring. A goal or run scored can do just that. And a coach should promote it.

Now, of course, if a team doesn't refocus afterwards, then a coach needs to step in and regain their attention. A coach can only put up with so much of a wide receiver dancing on the bench in front of a TV camera while his offensive unit is in a sideline huddle. The coach can always refocus players if he needs to during the game. John Wooden once said, "The bench is the best teacher in sports."

For the most part in sports, the celebrations that go on during games can only help a team's motivation and confidence. So much is said or written about momentum during games. The fact is that the momentum of a game often swings with the emotions of the teams playing. When a team is "pumped up," feeling confident that they're moving in the right direction, the momentum is often theirs.

Lesson from a Legend: Vince Lombardi

 Vince Lombardi was always known as a driver. He was a tough coach and relentless on his players. Referred to as "that son of a bitch" by many Packers, Lombardi was adamant in his position that nothing but victory would be tolerated. He became famous for his various quotes extolling just that.

However, as a former player himself, Lombardi knew what his players were going through. He knew that after a game, they needed to celebrate and to revel in the feeling of victory. He knew about the cases of beer at the back of the plane or the bus. He knew that certain players had the habit of living it up after games. Without publicly or officially acknowledging it, he let these celebrations happen. However, when practices resumed on Monday, it was back to business.

Lombardi was, along with Dallas Cowboys former coach Tom Landry, one of the NFL pioneers in the use of game film. He was always in position to point to what went right or wrong in the team's performance and with that of individual players. The ability to refocus the team was always at his disposal. In that respect, he could control for how long and to what extent his team celebrated their little victories.

The best example of Lombardi's use of this tactic occurred in 1960. In his second year as head coach of the Packers, who were only two years removed from their dismal 1-10-1 season, Lombardi took them to the NFL championship game. In an epic battle against the Philadelphia Eagles, the Packers' chances came down to a last-second drive. As quarterback Bart Starr's completed pass from the Eagles 22 yard line with a handful of seconds left on the clock turned into a sure scoring run, disaster struck them. An Eagle tackler, the only man left to beat, made an impossible tackle to end the game. The Packers lost 17-13.

After the game, the only surprise in the locker room was that there were no tears. The Packers had come from the bottom of the league to compete with the best, and they knew that all they had needed were a few more seconds. Lombardi gave a stirring speech. He stated that to him, there was a revelation in that loss. He said, "Perhaps you didn't realize that you could have won this game. But I think there's no doubt in your minds now. And that's why you will win it all next year. This will never happen again. You will never lose another championship." And they never did during Lombardi's reign.

The Coach as Manager: Small Victories Reinforce the Game Plan

In spite of many human resources professionals and authors imploring mid- to low-level managers to "celebrate little victories," this doesn't often happen. To many managers it doesn't seem right, and it certainly doesn't come naturally. "Only the end result matters," we are taught. It always seems too premature to ever talk of anything less than complete victory.

These managers worry, of course, that their employees will grow comfortable, complacent, and stop improving if a celebration follows every small success. They fear that after a celebration, it will be difficult to re-engage employees in the task at hand. Common thinking is that it's far easier, and more constructive, to continue to hold the carrot out in front of people and say, "You're not there yet. Keep trying."

Management styles that focus only on the end result would have the manager continue to push people without so much as a mention of any degree of success or progress. In fact, how many times has a manager been chastised by upper management for trying to celebrate a small success? All too frequently, a manager gets labeled as "soft" for attempting to reinforce positive behavior positively and often.

However, this is a completely different discussion if a group of individuals is focused not only on the end result, but also on the plan that will eventually get them there. A group of employees that is fully aware of the overall plan and the goals of the group will be able to recognize a small achievement as just that, one step forward. From the perspective of the overall plan, incremental gains become more noticeable. If the group has significant milestones identified on the path to their overall accomplishment, then the reason for celebrating one of those achievements is all the more justifiable. For this reason, the progress of the team should be measured and shared with team members, so that their position relative to the end result is always known. If celebrations are handled in this manner, then team members will always be reminded that they have not yet achieved the goal. Be prepared, however, that this may conflict with the management style that prefers to ignore opportunities for positive feedback until the end point has arrived.

We are told that goals must be placed on the horizon for us to see and pursue. However, the manager must realize and accept that an expedition to reach the horizon may result in a never-ending journey, especially in these days of stiff competition and "moving targets." If the game plan has been taught and understood and the celebration is in the context of that plan, a little emotional release can only help to reinforce the plan. All the more reason to allow and encourage the group to feel good about their progress. They should feed off of any positive source of energy they can find. Everyone needs to get reenergized at some point. A moment to feel good about their accomplishments can do that.

PUTTING THE LESSON IN ACTION

Throughout the early period of our efforts, I took an emotional beating from upper management for not achieving the results that they sought for my operation. Regardless of inherited shortcomings, I had the task of turning the place around. Our organization as a whole was seeking to climb from the basement of the industry up to the higher "world-class" echelons in only a couple of years. In the eyes of upper management, my team could not move fast enough.

There was no argument on my part that our challenge was necessary. I knew we had to move quickly and drive improvement. As a management team, we worked hard to create a game plan that would deliver the results that were necessary for the survival of our operation, as well as our own reputations as managers. The team had planned, prepared, and was busy executing.

As a group, we had our eye on the horizon, and we were moving in all the right directions. Our progress could be seen in a steady climb upward on all the charts. It was becoming obvious to all of us involved that we had a date with destiny. We began to feel encouraged that we were on the right track. As our performance became more defined and we began to hit significant milestones, I looked for opportunities to celebrate. While learning to walk is not the same as learning to run, it is still a major accomplishment.

I can remember having arguments with some members of upper management when I approached them on the subject of recognition. "You're not there yet," I was told. "You can't let them off the hook so easily." My management style was questioned, as was my intention. I can still remember walking off in anger, furious that my leaders in this multibillion dollar company were choking over my plans for a pizza lunch for a few hundred people that had blown another milestone out of the water.

On a number of other occasions I tried, in vain, to seek small rewards for my team's efforts. We continued to make significant improvements and even set records for the departments over and over again. And each time I looked for support in my celebratory efforts, I was met by disbelief that I did not "get the message the first time." So I began to find ways to recognize the departments on my own.

We had gone to great lengths to make the employees aware of what our overall goals were. We posted them in plain sight. We talked about them in meetings. We stressed them at every opportunity. I, therefore, was not concerned that these employees would settle back into complacency.

So we ate pizza. And donuts. I paid money out of my own pocket when I had to. At Christmas time, I personally bought gifts for all my management team. I wrote over a hundred different personal letters to key members of the team. I had signs created, plant messages printed, and personally shook people's hands. This went on over a period of a year.

And sure enough, the hundreds of people in my operation began to feed off of that recognition. Suddenly, there was a sense of enthusiasm, a feeling that we were onto something here. The team members themselves began paying more attention to the operation's performance. As I walked on the factory floor, employees would tell me what percentages we were scoring that day. Suddenly, the workplace became cleaner and brighter, as people began improving their work environment out of pride. While I had no way of confirming it, I also sensed that people were actually talking and socializing with each other more.

We hit the overall goal in the end. And what did I hear from upper management when we got there? "The goal has changed." So I bought more pizza.

CHAPTER 17

Treat Players Equally

---

*I DO NOT CARE IF YOU ARE WHITE OR BLACK or Irish
or Italian or Catholic or Jewish or liberal or
conservative. From this point on, I will treat you
all the same—like dogs.*

— BO SCHEMBECHLER
FORMER UNIVERSITY OF MICHIGAN FOOTBALL COACH
SPEAKING AT THE FIRST PRACTICE OF THE 1969 SEASON

THE COACH'S LESSON

I had a player on the Rockies who was our top goal scorer for each of the three years. He was overflowing with natural talent. Off the ice, however, he exhibited unpredictable behavior. He was kicked out of school, got into fights, hung out with bad crowds, and eventually became a father at the ripe age of nineteen. A great kid with a huge heart and a terrific personality, he had become a favorite of mine. The assistant coaches and I tried to steer him as best we could and to keep his mind where it should be.

During one of his irresponsible spells, he missed three practices in a row. That was bad enough, but the fact that he hadn't called any of the coaches was inexcusable. We always told the kids that they absolutely had to come to all practices, but if something came up, they had to call one of us beforehand. He had failed to do that and after three strikes, he was out in my book.

He showed up for the game following that string of missed practices, acting as if nothing had happened. He dressed as usual and was in his normal state of anxiety and excitement in the dressing room. Once the game began, however, I never called his name for any of the lines. And so he sat. And sat. After the first period had come to a close, I noticed that his shoulders had slumped with the realization that he was being "sat out." His teammates, one by one, would lean over to him and ask, "What's up?" He, of course, had no answer.

At some point near the end of the second period, I leaned over behind him and whispered in his ear, "If you can't come to practices like the other guys, then you can't play on *their* team. And if you don't respect me enough to call ahead of time to tell me, then you can't play on *my* team. You, one of the captains of this team, should know better." He turned his head toward the ice and continued to stew.

Now I happen to know that the worst thing for a player is to dress for a game, expecting to play, only to sit on the bench. A player would rather not be allowed to dress for the game. That avoids the emotional free fall that accompanies the first few minutes on the bench. It also averts the attention and embarrassment that comes with the stares of teammates, parents, and fans. In this case, given his stature as the most valuable player on the team, the message needed to hit home a lot harder than normal.

When we got into the dressing room after losing a close game that we could have won, I addressed the entire team about the incident. After reiterating the rules, describing what had happened in this case, I emphasized that sitting on the bench would be the penalty for missed practices, regardless of who the player was. The looks on the faces of the players were mixed. While there were some who thought I threw away a game to prove a point, there were others who looked at our assistant captain with disappointment that he had done something stupid and hurt the team overall. Regardless of their reactions, I never had any problems with respect to that team rule ever again.

Good Coaches Don't Show Favorites

The coach's relationship with his players may, at times, resemble the parent-child relationship. The coach recognizes the personalities of each individual and tries to coax something out of them in several different ways. The approach might differ from player to player. It may be a change in his manner of speaking, or using a humorous tone versus a professional one. Whatever the tactic, a coach must learn the best ways to communicate, teach, and nurture a group of different characters in any number of unique ways. Sounds just like a family, doesn't it?

As in the parent-child relationship, a coach must always avoid developing any favorites in the group. Instead, he must try to treat them all equally—what is good for one of them is good for all. The amount of attention can't vary drastically, lest anyone feel slighted. Praise needs to be spread around to all so that each player will feel encouraged. More important, from my perspective, is that discipline be dished out fairly and equally—what applies to one player should apply to all of them.

On a team that is striving to develop a sense of discipline in everything they do, the rules must be respected. If a coach has declared the rules well in advance, and the players all have understood the warnings, then a coach should expect that the rules set forth will be honored. If players break the rules, then they must be dealt with swiftly and without prejudice. The punishment should be predictable; consistent, fair, and should come as no surprise to anyone. This is vital to establishing any disciplined behavior or a sense of order amongst the players.

This is especially critical if the infraction has disrupted the team in any way, shape, or form. That makes it inexcusable. For any one player to impact his team by some disrespectful or irresponsible violation of a team policy should be intolerable for a coach. The urgency to deal with the player is heightened if the rest of the team has witnessed, or has any knowledge of, the offense.

Sometimes it is difficult not to play favorites. The true test of a coach's mettle will come when one of his best players breaks a team rule. It is understandably easier to discipline a marginal player, knowing that the ripple effect throughout the team may be minimal. However, disciplining one of the team's stars may put the entire team at a disadvantage at game time.

The eyes of the team move quickly from the violator to the judge. It is naive to think that they aren't waiting to see "how the coach is going to react to this one." How the coach deals with the star player will speak volumes to the other players. It will communicate either an intolerance of rule violations that transcends team status, or an inconsistent approach that smacks of double standards. For this reason alone, the coach must address the issue of infractions—no matter the transgressor.

Lesson from a Legend: Lou Holtz

 In both his years at the University of Arkansas and Notre Dame, Lou Holtz had incidents that, in his opinion, required him to take a firm stand. Holtz's teams always had guidelines for the personal conduct of players. These were embodied in his team's "Do Right" rule. Holtz was adamant early in every season that violation of this rule would not be tolerated.

While at the University of Arkansas during the 1977 season, Holtz's Razorbacks had just completed a 10-1 season and were headed for the Orange Bowl, one of the most prestigious post-season bowl games. The week before Christmas, Holtz was informed of an incident involving three of his best players. The infraction was unimportant to Holtz. What was important was the fact that the three players had violated the team's "Do Right" rule. Complicating matters for the coach was the fact that these three players had accounted for *78 percent of the team's touchdowns* that season. True to his form, as well as his warning to the team, Holtz suspended all three players from playing in the Orange Bowl game. Players, opponents, media, and alumni were all stunned by the move.

The incidents that followed became a national media event. The three players filed suit against the team, seeking an injunction against the suspension. The motion, defended by a pre-political career, young attorney named Bill Clinton, was turned down. And so the suspensions stood. Throughout the days leading up to the game, Holtz defended his actions to the media. He later stated matter-of-factly, "They simply made a bad decision. They chose not to play when they decided to behave badly." They broke the rules and were treated no differently than anyone else in that situation.

His Razorbacks went into the game as 24-point underdogs

against the Oklahoma Sooners. In fact, by game time, bookies wouldn't even take bets on the game—that's how heavily favored the Sooners were. A few days before the game, during a rousing meeting with the sullen players, Holtz challenged them to come up with reasons why they *could* win; after all, everyone knew why they couldn't. One by one, reasons were offered, each sparking new enthusiasm. After that session, he had successfully motivated them to prove all the pundits wrong. Arkansas then went on to upset Oklahoma and win the Orange Bowl by a surprising score of 31-6.

The Coach as Manager: Favoritism Destroys Team Unity

The manager faces many of the same group dynamics as the coach. Each employee or subordinate is unique. Each requires different tactics and approaches to help them succeed, but as a group, they must be treated equally.

In the workplace, many people assume favoritism is accompanied by more money, better assignments, promotions and, in general, a better life. The favored employee is the one more apt to get ahead. This, of course, is the kind of fuel that keeps office politics burning. In an environment where politics, back stabbing, and sabotage happens all too frequently, a manager must avoid showing favoritism at all costs.

Given the benefits of being in the boss's favor, employees watch carefully to see whom the manager holds in higher regard. It is only natural to expect them to do so. In the business world, those of us who are competitive are driven by many different motivators. The notion that another employee is getting an edge on us is only one of them. Any evidence of bias in the boss's actions attracts the attention of employees who are either disdainful or envious of it. Coworkers may then begin to question the motives of others and slowly grow untrusting of them. This can lead to decay of team unity and, eventually, the development of a dysfunctional work group.

Discipline can take many forms in the workplace. While suspension and discharges come to mind, it need not be that extreme. Likewise, the violation isn't normally a major breach of company policy. The infraction may be as simple as a disregard for a team norm. Regardless of the type of rule, the team members must recognize that violating any of the rules is unacceptable. And the manager must react swiftly and decisively, especially if the violator is one of his or her favorites.

Beware the Legal Ramifications of Double Standards

Managers must also keep in mind the legal ramifications of double standards in the workplace. In today's increasingly litigious society, it is imperative for managers to be more mindful than ever about the way they treat their employees. All too often, the appearance of bias and favoritism leads some employees to exercise discrimination laws to level what they perceive as an unequal playing field.

A manager in this day and age had better use a fair, even-handed approach to doling out punishment. More than ever before, he or she must discipline all employees equally if they break a rule or policy of the organization. As difficult as it may seem to punish someone who is a solid performer, the consequences of not doing so are all too great. Not only does a manager risk sending mixed signals about what is right, wrong, or punishable, but he or she also risks charges of unfair treatment. No matter what, the manager must deal with every infraction fairly and appropriately.

Order and regulation in the work environment will always be a necessity of a well-functioning organization. A group of people will rarely march together to a common beat in a common direction without it. This unity has to be the primary consideration of the manager. He or she is the one person who absolutely must be looking out for the best interests of the whole group. Consequently, it is the manager who must set the example that nothing comes before the welfare of the organization.

PUTTING THE LESSON IN ACTION

Even though our work environment is a high stress, high pressure one, it is still easy to be good friends with coworkers, bosses, and subordinates. It's difficult to spend so many hours together and not develop friendships or partiality to each other. For boss-subordinate relationships, that's fine, as long as professionalism is maintained. If it is not, however, favoritism can develop and quickly poison team camaraderie and harmony. This is not an easy lesson to learn, since favoritism is not an attribute that many of us are eager to own up to.

Through the years, a number of my team members have been my peers as well as personal friends outside of work. Overall, there were countless opportunities for me to favor any one of them over the majority of the team members. Of course, I thought I could manage it.

Likewise, I had developed a solid friendship with my immediate boss. We had worked together for many years and enjoyed a professional work relationship that was based on mutual respect for each other. But we were good friends outside of work as well. As a result, there were times when I tried to exercise some imaginary privileges that I thought I had as a result of our friendship. And yes, my peers noticed it and would comment. But it meant nothing, I thought.

One day, however, that notion came crashing down on me. I was called into my boss's office to discuss a purchase I had approved—new cubicles and desks for the production offices of our assembly operations. The supervisors had long complained about their dilapidated workspace. I felt that the amount of money to be spent was acceptable and justifiable. And besides the team was performing well—it was the least I could do for them. Unfortunately, my boss' superior had previously decreed that there would be a temporary moratorium on the purchase of any new furniture.

During an excruciating fifteen minutes, I was raked over the coals for my actions. My superior claimed that I had taken a few liberties as a result of my cockiness. I disagreed. In fact, I was incredulous. My departments were at the height of their success. I was delivering results that were outstanding! I refused to take the reprimand seriously. "How can I possibly be getting in trouble for this?" I wondered aloud with a smirk on my face. That's when all hell broke loose. If the seriousness of the matter wasn't apparent to me before, it certainly was now. I had some privileges rebuked while also being threatened with a number of forms of discipline. I walked out stunned.

It took me days to settle down. Over and over, I replayed the meeting in my mind, trying to find some explanation for it. I felt betrayed by a personal friend. Surely he didn't mean it. He must have been trying to scare me. After avoiding my boss for the better part of two days, I finally approached him to talk about the incident.

In an enlightening few words, the picture came into focus. He said, "It doesn't matter who you are or how good you are. If you break the rules, you have to pay the penalty. I would do no differently with any of the other managers that work for me. How do you think they would feel if they saw you get away with this?" I left with my head down and his words crowding my mind. For some reason, they sounded familiar.

It didn't take long for me to recall using the same argument, and possibly the same words, at the arena with my Rockies. I realized that I was violating at work the same philosophy of equality I insisted on enforcing as a coach. And, of course, after further consideration, I realized that I was treating my own work team with varying degrees of favoritism. I was guilty on many counts. I began to pay attention to how and when I enforced rules. Sure enough, there were differences. Some people received preferential treatment. And yes, I could tell that other team members knew it, too. I was humbled by the recognition that I was vulnerable to bouts of favoritism. And so the lesson was taught and my development as a manager continued.

CHAPTER 18

Always Remember Why You Won or Lost

Most coaches study the films when they lose. I study them when we win—to see if I can figure out what I did right.

— Paul "Bear" Bryant
FORMER FOOTBALL COACH, University of Alabama

THE COACH'S LESSON

I always took time after the games to talk with the Rockies. After they changed out of their uniforms and settled down, I called for silence and launched into a post-game discussion. Win, loss, or tie, they got the same analysis. I reviewed the team's play by comparing it to the techniques we used in practice. If we strayed from our game plan, or tried to play a style of hockey that was not our own, I emphasized that. I wanted to mold the thoughts that would accompany them on their ride home.

Normally, after a game, players are caught up in their own thoughts. As a player, I knew that. You sit there, rewinding plays in your head, mentally bemoaning missed opportunities or celebrating successful plays. It's a moment of individual reckoning for the player. I would never dissuade that. I assumed it would happen, and I encouraged it with one-on-one comments to players regarding their game. But I also wanted the team to reflect on the larger group's success or failure in executing the game plan. I wanted the smaller groups to reflect on their play as a unit. I found that constantly referring to group play in the post-game locker room emphasized the team aspect of our game at a time when players were normally reflecting on their own personal play.

While keeping my comments brief, I always talked of the players' performances in the context of the game plan and our preparation. The good, well-executed performances were easy to speak to. For example, "Damon and Garreth, your work in front of our net was exactly what we said we needed and wanted to do. It was just as we practiced it."

Discussing the poor performances required a little more tact. I found that if I avoided any personal comments and kept my message grounded in the game plan and our preparation, my words sounded more objective. Such as, "You guys on the penalty-killing line need to work on the positioning in our zone. Remember the formations we were practicing. We talked about how we needed to avoid bunching up in the middle of the ice if we started to panic, and tonight we panicked a lot."

I applied the same strategy with individual members of the team. Many times in these post-game reviews I mentioned particular plays made by single players. I always felt it was important to touch on the play of some individuals so that the remaining players could relate the contribution that an individual made to the team's effort. This also reinforced the importance of each role on the team.

Finally, before we all headed home, I left them with a single thought. I highlighted one aspect of our overall play that directly contributed to the game's result. I might, for example, point out how well we covered the opposing players while we were defending the front of our own net on defense. I would ask them to think about how they contributed, good or bad, to that aspect. Knowing how a player's mind works, I knew that they would rehash many of the game's moments over the next few hours. It was always my hope that at some point during that period of time, they would reflect on how their individual efforts contributed to the success or failure of the team and alter their approach to the next game accordingly.

In the next practice following a game, I would gather them all together for a talk. Here I would again interpret our play in the previous game, with particular emphasis on what we didn't do well. That would then lead into my explanation of what plays or strategies we would be working on during practice. My thinking was that the more parallels I could draw between what we needed to improve on during game time and what we were actually practicing between games, the more effort I might get out of them. It was important for them to understand how the lessons applied to the games.

Learn How to Lose

Games provide sports teams with a unique learning opportunity. For this reason, no game should ever be allowed to fade into memory without first gaining some lessons from it. Any team that is intent on improving will use each game as a chance to critique, reinforce, and reward itself. This should be a must for every team, regardless of the outcome of the game.

Many teams spend a good portion of the next day reviewing the previous day's game films. They may also find themselves reliving certain details during the following practices. Or they may simply spend a useful period of time in the locker room, immediately following the game, rehashing what happened in the game and learning from it.

The purpose of this exercise should never be lost on the team. Many coaches through the years have agreed that "In order to win, a team must first learn how to lose." That's a thought that doesn't make sense when you first think or hear it. How do you "learn how to lose"? Well, think about what's involved with losing. Mistakes are made. Opportunities are squandered. Players fail to execute assignments properly. Most importantly though, lessons are learned. The players have to dig into the details of their own play, as well as that of the team's. They must be able to identify what they did well and what they did poorly in order to improve from that point forward. They must be able to associate aspects of their own individual play to the results of the game. Losing naturally creates the conditions for an introspective analysis.

Analyze the Wins, Too

Winning also teaches valuable lessons—although many teams fail to stop and consider them amidst the rump slapping, high-fiving, and "good games." It's too easy for coaches to say, "Good effort. That's the way to do it, now hit the showers." In a losing situation, that same coach would probably go into great detail about what went wrong in an effort to drive home the lessons learned. What might be the response if a coach spent the same amount of time, in the same amount of detail, analyzing a win? There will always be aspects of a team's play in a winning effort that can be used to reinforce what a coach has been trying to teach. It's a perfect opportunity to use an "I told you so," with a positive spin: if the players carried out the game plan and used the plays and skills learned in practice, then a win is proof that the coach's strategy is valid.

Since this is an important exercise for a team, it is up to the coach to make time for this reflection after games. Better yet, if a coach can make it a regular activity, then the learning response of the team can become more natural and reflexive. They might even subconsciously expect it. A coach should try to make this discussion a regular part of the post-game talk. It should also make its way into the next practice or team meeting.

Lesson from a Legend: Bill Walsh

 Known as one of the best motivators of the modern-day NFL, Bill Walsh enjoyed tremendous success with the San Francisco 49ers. Through the years, he built solid game plans and encouraged players, even drove some of them, to reach their highest potential. What is amazing, however, is that the organization that Walsh helped to create and mold continued to succeed after Walsh retired, including winning one more Super Bowl. It was a testament to the skills, environment, motivation, and team spirit that Walsh established, all interwoven with the confident, professional, and classy style that defined the 49ers.

To maintain that winning form over a period of many years, Walsh took the post-game reflection to a new level. He, like most coaches, was devoted to analyzing the game afterwards. His strict game-week schedule began with regular review of film from the previous game and dissecting the overall execution. This activity would first involve assistant coaches, then later, the players themselves. Each player's execution was graded, and scores were compiled in an effort to quantify and compare performances. Players would gather in their functional groups—offense, defense, special teams, etc.—and join in the analysis.

Win or lose, Walsh held to the same guidelines in his

treatment of the team. He made sure that all team standards were upheld, even during a losing streak. The staff kept the game plan's execution as the primary focus. Losses were not personalized. Victories were celebrated, but only for the moment. Walsh's own personal emphasis was on the details— of preparation as well as execution. And everything always returned to the game plan.

Proving the worthiness of his Hall of Fame stature, Walsh took winning to a new level and was able to sustain it throughout the decade of the '80s. He took his approach to reflecting and learning after each game and expanded it to an unprecedented activity performed after each season had ended. Regardless of the 49ers' end result, Walsh led them through the same type of exercises. He, of course, already had the assistant coaches working through their analysis of the previous season, using many of the same post-game methods to grade performance and to assess strengths and weaknesses. Walsh would then hold team meetings throughout the off-season, gathering the players, sometimes in groups, sometimes individually, for sessions that would revolve around past performance and future expectations. Players would watch videotapes of footage that showed both outstanding and poor performances. Throughout this off-season period, Walsh would always attach every lesson, every performance critique, and all future expectations to the team game plan. While this effort by a coach may be easy to understand after a losing season, consider that Walsh's 49ers went through this after each of their Super Bowl victories, as well.

The Coach as Manager: Emotions Sideline Useful Analysis

While it seems a natural and sensible activity, reflecting on our "wins and losses" in business is not all that common. Furthermore, talking about our successes and failures is such a lopsided concept in the workplace. We spend plenty of time talking about why we "lost," but never enough time reflecting on why we "won." Here again, it is way too easy for a manager to shrug off a good effort as "that's what I pay you for."

Think about how much time we spend talking about things that went wrong at work. Worse yet, think about the tone in which we discuss it. We yell at people who have failed. We chastise those that have erred, saying, "You should have known better." Too often, we give feedback that is more emotional than analytical. And, the feedback rarely relates back to specific tasks and assignments as they relate to the overall game plan.

How often do we turn these reflective opportunities into lessons learned? How often do we allow the education and training process to overpower our frustration and anger? The truth is, not often. We sit through useless meetings, perform redundant tasks, use burdensome systems, or continue to do things because "that's the way it's always been done." And we rarely reflect on how we are "executing at game time." We don't take the time to assess our own performance as a team, or as individuals, in the context of our overall game plan.

If individual assignments and executable tasks are detailed out, communicated, understood, and practiced, then the expectations are no secret. Performance evaluations can easily be founded on the comparison between these expectations and the actual execution of the work. For the coach concerned with keeping the work group motivated, the game plan will be the basis for objective critiques of performance. The more detail in the plan, the easier it will be to review people's performances. However, without the presence of an overall plan or thorough preparation to refer to, most constructive criticism comes across as subjective. As a result, people take it personally, thinking, "I can never do anything right in her eyes. She hates me." When an employee reacts in that manner, the chances of the manager's comments having the desired effect become slim.

Many managers fail to realize that evaluating performances can be done quickly, more often, and much more effectively, if an overall game plan exists and is talked about regularly, practiced frequently, and referred to often. Remember that a good game plan will detail roles, assignments, and executable tasks. And if you're talking about it regularly as a group or one-on-one, then the expectations are constantly being reinforced. So when a positive or negative result occurs that warrants equal reinforcement, it can happen on a real-time basis in a manner that can be informal and quick. There will be no need to dig up the personnel file to retrieve previous performance reviews or signed documents that pledge, "I promise to work harder, faster, stronger…" Instead, it can be a comment at the coffee machine or a statement in a meeting.

Success Is Not a Silent Game

When was the last time you spent a significant amount of time discussing an effort that went well with your team members? In fact, try to remember an opportunity that any manager took to discuss, in any amount of detail, the positive efforts of a group after a successful accomplishment. We're not talking about a pat on the back or some formal recognition. We're looking for "post-game analysis." We're talking about any time where the focus of the reflection was to learn and to reinforce an overall plan. Unfortunately, managers are much less likely to reinforce lessons after successes than after failures.

Talking about successes and reinforcing desired performance is a tool that absolutely *should* be part of a manager's repertoire. It's the stuff that a learning, improving organization must feed on to thrive and grow. And you'll find that when the work group gets excited and begins to feed off of the energy generated by their own improvements, they will begin to look forward to these opportunities to critique both the good and bad results of their efforts.

PUTTING THE LESSON IN ACTION

I remember the first time I employed this tactic at work. We had been on a rocky road of improvement. We could see that we were on the right track and destined for success, but a successful day's worth of production was always just barely out of our reach. Then one day it happened. We burst past all of our goals and delivered a world-class production run, with throughput and quality numbers that were close to perfect.

I walked up to the engineers and supervisors of the engine assembly line after the shift and joined in the congratulations. However, after a few moments of backslapping, I moved the group into a conference room. There I asked them all one question: "What did you do differently in order to have such a great run today?" They looked at me strangely, since this was the one day they would not have expected to answer any questions after the shift ended. Of course, their immediate answers were "Nothing, everything just ran well today."

After further questioning, they started to relive the details of the day. We drew comparisons to the behavior on previous days. Eventually, we began to identify actions that had been performed that day, as well as in the recent past few days, that all had contributed to our success. In the end, we compiled a list of actions that all had some positive impact on our performance. The smiles and nods of some of the supervisors were even larger, since now they realized that they had indeed played a role in their success. I appealed to them to "remember why you won."

The next day, I met them at the beginning of the shift for a pep talk. I reminded them of each of the actions that they had identified the day before. I asked them to pledge that they would perform those same actions that day. This review of our daily progress went on for a number of weeks. Eventually, it became a habit for us to always "remember why we won or lost."

Over that period, I saw the greatest improvement in the performance of the production management team. Since they were recording successful production runs on a more frequent basis, and they were relating it to their own actions, a sense of pride began to develop. Soon, they were running on all eight cylinders as their own level of performance had ratcheted up.

I transferred this same approach to the engineering groups, which I also managed. Their goals were not as easy to measure, since they are really a support group by nature. However, by pointing to the increased performance of the line, the successful implementation of equipment improvements, and the timely installation of new equipment, they were able to identify their contributions to the success of the operation. Eventually, they reacted just as positively. Within a few weeks, they were referring to past actions that had a positive impact, reminding each other to continue them. They were reinforcing their own positive behavior.

Over time, all the groups began to think proactively in this manner. I would get answers before asking the questions. *They* would begin discussing what they did differently that day that they believed helped. Even more constructive, they would willingly offer the same information to each other without anyone walking away with hurt feelings.

I had always wanted to be part of a "learning" organization. However, to create one, the people on the team had to drop their guard, open their minds, and challenge themselves to learn. They had to openly discuss their performance as a group. First, they had to realize that there is no need for personal defenses among peers who share the same goals and desires. Then they needed to adopt an open-minded approach to performance discussions so that constructive criticism could have a positive effect. Finally, they needed to challenge themselves to learn and treat that activity as an important individual contribution to the entire team's development.

I began to use the game plan as the foundation for all my comments. The Rockies responded well when I focused on our game plan, maintained an objective and impersonal tone, and balanced the positive and negative critiques—so why not try it on my work team?

My team members at work reacted predictably well as I changed my approach. My remarks on individuals' behaviors or performances were always based on "What we said we wanted/needed to do to execute the plan properly." By making a point to balance positive and negative comments, I was able to maintain people's focus without deflating anyone. In fact, it was amazing how many people were "starving" to hear positive feedback. Since my team members knew that I was noticing and appreciating their good work, my comments on their less-than-good work seemed easier to accept.

As the team's capacity to accept and internalize regular, objective feedback increased, I introduced this activity in the group setting. I began to look for opportunities to discuss our performances as a team. When I sensed enough of their collective guards being dropped, I solicited comments on my own performance by critiquing myself in front of them. This normally was enough to open the floor to the kind of introspective discussion the group needed.

By transferring my coaching skills to the workplace, I had helped create an organization that truly learned from both failure and success. They challenged themselves daily to become better, no matter how well they had done the day before.

How to Analyze the Game

➤ **Step 1: Determine if necessary milestones and results are being achieved.**

To determine if your game plan is succeeding or not, it's important to measure your progress on a regular basis. To do so:

❑ Review your game plan pyramid. Ask yourself: Are you and your team achieving the necessary milestones and results with respect to:

____ Achieving team objectives,

____ Implementing work unit methods and systems,

____ Executing individual assignments and tasks,

❑ If not, determine why. Ask:

____ What problems need to be addressed?

____ What lessons have we learned?

____ Are these the right objectives, methods and systems, or individual assignments and tasks?

____ Is something wrong with our approach?

____ Does the team's skill-building plan need to be adjusted?

____ Are there motivational or environmental barriers to team, work unit, and/or individual performance?

➤ **Step 2: Build on your success!**

For each area of success, be sure to ask:

❑ What roles were executed well by team members?

❑ Which methods or systems delivered the desired results?

❑ How did the team's playing style contribute to our success?

❑ What modifications were made to successfully adjust to unforeseen problems?

❑ What are the keys to our success?

❑ What actions do we want to repeat?

As the Lights of the Arena Dim...

THE PLAYERS MAKE THE MANAGER. It's never the other way around.

— GEORGE "SPARKY" ANDERSON
FORMER MAJOR LEAGUE BASEBALL MANAGER,
CINCINNATI REDS, DETROIT TIGERS

Whether coaches or managers are behind the steering wheel, the car rides home are the same. As they leave their offices or the playing fields, the brain's cogs will spin. While trying to remember what time a child's soccer practice is, they will also question if they made the right decision a few hours earlier. Plans to finalize the summer vacation will bounce off of details of the business plan. A mental note to call Mom will be posted next to the one reminding the driver to discuss poor performance with a failing employee. There are always second thoughts and harsh personal critiques. Few of us ever believe that we have done everything that we possibly could as well as we possibly could have.

The fact is that we, like our employees and players, are only human. We have good days and bad. Sometimes we're extremely focused; other times we're distracted. There may not be too many of us that are consistently excellent. Personalities sometimes play a larger role in success and failure than they should ever be allowed to.

This daily dose of personal reality is all the more reason to base a management approach on a well-founded, organized methodology. We need structure to our management style for the same reasons that we need structure in the game plan for our employees—to maintain focus where it may not naturally exist. Basing a manager's organizational approach on a detailed game plan will achieve that focus for both employees and managers alike.

The game plan is essential to the learning cycle of the team. It is the one constant that bridges the organization's planning, development, execution, and performance reinforcement phases. Additionally, the common theme will maintain consistency in a manager's message. Allowing that game plan to be woven throughout the learning cycle of an organization will only proliferate opportunities to focus employees. With constant reinforcement and repetitious lessons, the game plan will gradually work its way into the bloodstream of a team. And with it, the manager's behavior will become more consistent as the messages begin to repeat themselves.

In the end, that's all we really want. We want to be in a position to help our teams. We want to be a source of guidance and support. If we can be a positive influence in an overall team's success, then we have performed our role. If we can do it consistently and fairly in a manner that garners respect, then we personally have succeeded. And in the end, we will be a part of a championship team that we ourselves helped to create.

In my office, I keep a picture of the Detroit Rockies. It was the team picture from our last year together. It sits next to the gold medal from the Can/Am tournament that we won in Lake Placid, NY during that one magical week. As you can imagine, many curious eyes have stared at that picture, momentarily surprised at the obvious image. When people ask about the framed picture and the medal, I tell them that it is my diploma from the greatest school of management I could have ever attended. It was an education that I wasn't looking for at the time, but haven't forgotten since.

It's been a number of years since that period of personal transformation. My work teams have since changed, the unfortunate but usual product of success. I have been moved to different assignments, as have most of my team members. The people who achieved so much for my teams then are achieving for other managers now. They are now a group of individuals who openly acknowledge that it is possible to experience the feelings of individual fulfillment and accomplishment while being a member of a larger team.

They recount to others their experience of job satisfaction, team camaraderie, and synergy, while feeling as if they actually were making a difference. They have become "preachers" of a better way to work together. Those that are now supervising their own teams have become leaders in their own right.

When I bump in to many of them now, they all have great recollections of our times together. So many of them can quote our accomplishments, resurrecting memories of all the performance measurements we had improved. Everyone seems to remember just how strong our team spirit was and how invincible they felt about our ability to achieve any of our goals against any challenge. But what stands out in my mind most are two common observations expressed by them: The first is that they loved the feeling that everyone was pointed in the same direction, each doing his or her part for the team. The second is that they felt that those were some of the happiest times in their careers. Those moments are what I, as a manager, live for.

Luckily for me, one of the people I still bump into quite often is Alex Gaston. Whether we are reliving past memories or catching up on news of the guys, my moments with Alex serve as a reminder to me of where some of my management roots lead. He and George Adams are now coaching again. Many years ago, they were thrust into a coaching role because their kids' team needed a coach. Now they do it simply because of the size of their hearts. Gloria Myers has retired from being a team manager to simply concentrate on being *only* a mother, a college student, and a career woman. They are exceptional people who together as their own team were outstanding role models for me. Much of the success of the Detroit Rockies is attributable to them.

And the guys? What can I say about them? I can't call them boys anymore since they're all young men now (not to mention the fact that they're all bigger than I am). My memories of them bring back the smile to my face that can only be put there by a bunch of teenaged boys being just that. Individually, they had character. Together, they were dynamite. They were close to each other in a way that can only be compared with a loving family. There was laughter, energy, and life in any room in which they were collected. They were, and continue to be, a special group.

Now, years later, they are all doing exceptionally well. They have become the men we had hoped they would be. Their lives have led them down different paths and in various directions across different states. Many of them went on to university. One joined the air force. Some of them now have wives and homes. They are all busy with jobs and careers and families, all the things that their coaches told them they would need to be prepared for.

While many of them were exceptional hockey players, none of them went too far with their loved sport. While three of them went on to play junior hockey, the remainder, for the most part, are playing in recreational leagues now. While George, Alex, and I had always thought that a couple of the guys were good enough to have been scouted for colleges, we were also realistic in the knowledge that not many scouts ever made it to the northwest neighborhoods of Detroit.

But what I am most impressed with about them is not *what* they are doing now, but rather *who* they have become. They all share values, maturity, and pride that are a credit to the parents, grandparents, and guardians who nurtured them through some challenging years. When I speak to them, they are respectful, open-minded, and appreciative of our years together.

Our reunions are emotional. I love every minute I can spend with them, especially since I can joke around with them more freely now. We laughed a lot during our years together. And we all grew up a lot. It was an experience during which the group made the individual a better person. As they have matured, they look back at those years differently. They recognize that we had something special and that we accomplished much more than simply winning a few hockey games. And in an act that continues to catch me off guard emotionally, they express appreciation for the time that Alex, George, Gloria, and I spent with them. In fact, in what may be the biggest compliment, four of them are involved in coaching hockey teams themselves.

They too will discover all the challenges and joys of coaching a team. I hope their experience is to them what it was for me—a catalyst for personal change. The impact of my time with the Rockies extends through my managerial experience and my penchant for leadership roles, and reaches down into an emotional level that defines who I am. I have become a better manager because of the Rockies. But more importantly, I have become a better person. That can be the impact of leading a team of people to achieve what they collectively want to achieve.

In his book about Vince Lombardi, David Maraniss writes about Lombardi's contribution to the team in the context of the quality of his players. He says, "If Lombardi found the best in his players, their performance in the end was limited by what the best could be." It is a simple statement that captures best what a coach's challenge encompasses. We can lead a group of individuals toward our goals, but in the end, it will be the team that achieves them. We begin with potential; what emerges is up to us.

The Greatest Lesson

*WINNING IS IMPORTANT, but if that's all that
matters, you're not looking at it the right way.*

— MIKE KRZYZEWSKI
BASKETBALL COACH, DUKE UNIVERSITY

At Jack Adams Arena, where the Detroit Hockey Association skated, I learned one valuable lesson. I learned this lesson gradually. It was taught by my senses and my emotions. It was the greatest lesson learned in all of my years of coaching.

As I drove to the arena past broken down cars, vagrants walking the streets, and boarded up homes; as I passed parents and grandparents waiting for their kids at the community center; as I watched volunteers work countless hours with the elderly and with children who were not their own; as I listened to some of my boys tearfully tell stories of absent fathers and dead friends; as I tried to understand the anger and rage that comes out of a sixteen-year-old boy on the ice during a game; and as I learned to love Alex Gaston, George Adams, Gloria Myers, and all of the other parents who desperately tried to keep the team going throughout the years for the sake of their kids, I learned that it was never about winning hockey games.

In work, as in sports, there is always something more important than the game.

Robert Evangelista

The Business of Winning
of
Winning — Appendix

THE GAME PLAN PYRAMID

Use this template and the following Coach's Playbooks to create your own winning game plan at work.

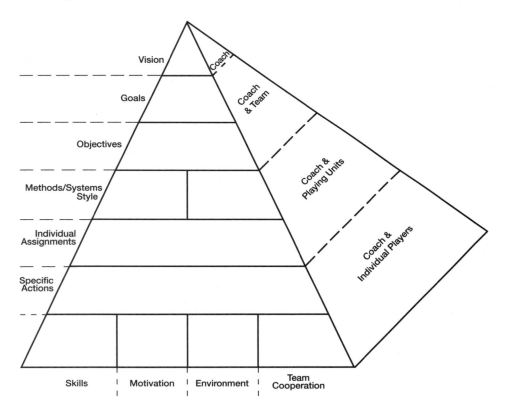

How You Can Create a Winning Game Plan

GOALS

➤ **Step 1: Set your department's goals.**

Use the *vision* communicated from higher management to develop your department's goals. Whether higher management has dictated your department's goals to you or you are developing them, make sure they are:

___ **Ambitious, yet attainable**—The goals should force the group to reach beyond what they normally achieve, but must also be within their reach. Goals must also have a chance to succeed: Your team must not only be capable of achieving the goals, but you must be in a position to support your team in achieving them.

___ **Customer driven**—The goals must not only meet the needs and requirements of your customers, but they also must impact your customers positively or the effort will be wasted.

___ **Competitor focused**—Assess the performance of the competition, especially those factors leading to your competitors' success. By establishing your department's goals, you should be challenging your competition to a race for customers and market share.

___ **Relevant to your organization's vision**—The goals must be in direct support of the overall vision or your efforts won't help your organization become or achieve what it desires.

___ **In line with your organization's values**—Achieving your goals should never compromise the values of your organization.

➤ **Step 2: Share the goals with your team.**

For the goals you have identified, use the following checklist to share the goals with your team. Don't assume team members will know what to do without specific direction tied to goals.

❑ Paint a picture of how achieving the goal will not only help the organization but also the team and the individual players. To do this, consider:

___ Leading your team in a visioning exercise. If the goal were being achieved, how would the team be operating? What kinds of things would be happening? What would the situation look like?

❑ Give team members a chance to react. The goal may seem impossible to them at first. Allow them to express these feelings. After all, if they never accept the goal, they'll never accomplish it. If team members have trouble accepting the goals, try this approach:

___ Create an open dialogue with the team to explore all of the obstacles they believe might prevent the achievement of the goal.

___ Help the team see these obstacles as challenges to be overcome.

___ Brainstorm on ways to overcome each obstacle by working with the team to identify their unique attributes—the specific characteristics that will help them accomplish the department's goals.

OBJECTIVES

➤ **Step 1: Work with your team to set objectives.**
For each goal you identified, work with your team to set objectives that are specific, measurable accomplishments that must be achieved in order to reach the goal. Consider such factors as:

❑ Time frame

❑ How much you need to increase or decrease specific productivity, sales, quality levels, etc.

❑ Numerical targets you need to hit

➤ **Step 2: For each objective you identify, perform a *gap analysis*.**
A gap analysis will help you establish the specific actions you and your team need to take to achieve each objective. To do this:

❑ Identify the specific objectives that your team is accomplishing today.

❑ Identify the specific objectives that your team needs to accomplish.

❑ Identify the differences between what your team is accomplishing today and what they need to accomplish to reach the stated objectives.

❑ Identify all of the obstacles that could prevent your team from achieving the stated objectives.

METHODS/SYSTEMS & PLAYING STYLE

➤ **Step 1: Brainstorm on new methods and systems that will overcome each obstacle.**
For each obstacle that is within your ability to control, identify the best solution to eliminate the obstacle. To help with this brainstorming session:

- ❑ Consider the methods and systems being used by other organizations.
- ❑ Review the methods and systems previously used by your department or organization.
- ❑ Ask yourself and your team: If all of these methods and systems were in place, would we be likely to achieve our goals?

➤ Step 2: Define your team's playing style.

As you work through this exercise, gauge the team's manner and mindset, as well as their group and individual strengths and weaknesses. This will help you identify the team's *playing style*, which will be important when you reach Step 3.

- ❑ Identify your team's current playing style.
- ❑ Identify the type of playing style you'll need to meet your goals. To do this, build on your team's strengths.
- ❑ Communicate the desired playing style to your team. Be explicit and clear about your expectations.
- ❑ Reinforce the new playing style whenever possible.

➤ Step 3: Select the new method(s) and system(s).

Select the combination of method(s)/system(s) that best match your team's playing style and are the most feasible to implement.

PLAYING STYLE

- ❑ Compare each new method and system to your team's playing style.
- ❑ If a method won't work because of team style, first try to find a method that better fits your team's playing style.
- ❑ If you can't find a method/system that matches your team's playing style, you may have to take action to change the style. This is a drastic step; be sure it's worth it!

FEASIBILITY

Consider such factors as:

- ❑ Manpower
- ❑ Time
- ❑ Budget
- ❑ Other necessary resources

INDIVIDUAL ASSIGNMENTS

➤ Step 1: Map out the *process flow*.

For each method/system, identify the sequence of steps/actions needed to implement it.

- ❏ Note the critical steps, sequences, deadlines, and communication that will need to occur.

- ❏ Identify what the decision points are and when they should come into play. Be sure to describe the resulting actions as well.

- ❏ Include checkpoints to ensure that the method/system is being implemented correctly.

➤ Step 2: Create the individual assignments.

Based upon your analysis of the process flow, develop specific executable assignments for each individual on your team. To do this:

- ❏ Identify each work unit and/or individual to be involved.

- ❏ Assign responsibility for each executable.

SPECIFIC ACTIONS

➤ Step 1: Define individual executable actions.

Create job instructions for groups and individuals that are based on the assignments you made. Don't forget to:

- ❏ Break all assignments down into actions that can be taught, practiced, executed, and evaluated.

- ❏ Document all required actions.

➤ Step 2: Define your expectations.

By documenting your expectations for each action, you will find it easier to review with employees on a regular basis. The documented job instructions and expectations can also serve as the basis for future performance reviews.

- ❏ For each required action, specify your expectations with regard to:

  ___ Timing requirements

  ___ Responsibility and accountability

  ___ Decisions to be made

  ___ Standardized tasks

  ___ Guidelines for conduct

  ___ Quality of work

How to Develop Your Players Into a Championship Team

SKILLS

➤ **Step 1: Identify skill requirements.**

For each process flow you developed in Coach's Playbook 1, list the essential skill requirements for each individual, as well as for the team as a whole. Be sure to:

❑ Be as specific as possible. The skill requirements you identify should:

___ Be observable.

___ Be targeted specifically to your team members' jobs (e.g., in addition to a general knowledge of tax laws and accounting, an accountant needs to know the specific payroll system and payroll schedule of his or her organization).

___ Include skills needed for your work units and your entire team to work well together (e.g., listening skills, communication skills, etc.).

___ Include both complex skills and fundamental skills (the "absolutely must do wells"). Don't assume that people know how to perform the basics.

➤ **Step 2: Prepare development plans.**

For each individual and work unit, as well as the team as a whole:

❑ Identify any skill gaps that exist (i.e., skills that are needed that don't already exist—again, don't forget to consider both basic as well as complex skills).

❑ List options for developing each of the deficient skills (e.g., coaching/ mentoring, training programs, on-the-job training, practice, role playing, simulations, etc.).

❑ Develop a skill-building plan for each individual and work unit, and for the team as a whole.

MOTIVATION AND ENVIRONMENT

➤ Step 1: Identify other barriers to performance.

For each individual, work unit, and team:

❑ Identify any motivational issues that might prevent your employees from meeting performance expectations. Ask yourself:

___ What might make people not want to do what is needed to execute the game plan?

___ What can be done to make them want to execute the game plan? To inspire them?

❑ Identify any environmental obstacles that might prevent your employees from meeting performance expectations (e.g., ergonomics, resources, equipment, authority, time, process, etc.)

❑ Plan strategies to address each motivational and/or environmental barrier you identify.

TEAM COOPERATION

➤ Step 1: Clarify performance expectations regarding team cooperation.

Your entire team needs to know exactly what your expectations are with respect to teamwork.

❑ Lead them in a visioning exercise by encouraging your team to share their thoughts and ideas about teamwork, describe potential obstacles that could prohibit them from working effectively together as a team, and offer suggestions for creating an environment of team cooperation.

❑ Once the visioning exercise is over, be sure to openly summarize your team's agreed-upon definition of team cooperation and the specific responsibilities each team member has in helping to achieve your team's common vision.

➤ Step 2: Create an environment of open communication.

To help pave the way toward true team cooperation, it's imperative that you establish an environment of trust, honesty, and fairness. The best way is by opening up a two-way stream of communication with your team members. You can do this by:

❑ Involving team members in planning and problem-solving activities.

❑ Providing each team member with individual airtime.

❑ Treating mistakes and problems as learning experiences.

- ❏ Being open about your own weaknesses and mistakes.
- ❏ Inviting constructive comments, opinions, and advice from team members.
- ❏ Keeping feedback and group discussions constructive and non-personal.
- ❏ Communicating "negative" feedback privately. Never chastise any individual in front of the group.

COACH'S PLAYBOOK 3

How to Become a
Highly Effective Sideline Manager

➤ **Step 1: Recognize when it's game time.**

Game time refers to:

❑ Any time when you are **not** planning, preparing, teaching, or learning. Conversely, it is any time you are doing, implementing, or executing.

❑ An event, action, or activity that:

___ Can't be interrupted.

___ You have planned or prepared for.

___ Is either the executable action listed in the game plan or is crucial to the success of the game plan.

➤ **Step 2: Understand that your role as manager at game time is different from any other time.**

Here are some tips to help you become a highly effective sideline manager.

DON'T...

❑ Lose objectivity by getting emotionally involved in a project, task, or undertaking.

❑ Attempt to teach while employees are trying to execute. (Remember that the added pressure of game time performance can minimize the impact of your lessons on your team.)

❑ Try to correct mistakes. Save this for the next appropriate learning opportunity unless your employees are jeopardizing the game plan irreparably. In many cases (such as when practice or lengthy discussions are required), it would be ineffective to attempt to correct mistakes during game time.

❑ Otherwise interrupt the execution of the plan.

❑ Be an unnecessary distraction.

❑ Make corrections based primarily on "how I would've done it."

DO...

- ❑ Analyze the actions of your staff and your team's progress toward the overall objective (save your analysis and share it with your team only when the action has subsided).

- ❑ Make necessary adjustments and corrections to keep your team aligned, but do so unobtrusively and only when you know that you can make an impact.

- ❑ Be available as a resource.

- ❑ Be a source of guidance, advice, and motivation.

- ❑ Reinforce the game plan whenever possible.

- ❑ Reinforce positive observations whenever possible.

- ❑ Keep an eye on your identified opponents.

- ❑ Plan the next "down time" learning opportunity.

- ❑ Assess the support structure that you've developed (what's working and what's not working as expected).

- ❑ Look for ways to remove obstacles for employees.

- ❑ Maintain discipline and adherence to the game plan by unobtrusively maintaining the team's focus on the game plan and reemphasizing unit responsibilities and individual assignments.

- ❑ Step in when an employee has lost emotional control or is otherwise acting contrary to the team playing style in a way that is compromising the execution of the game plan.

COACH'S PLAYBOOK 4

How to Analyze Your Game

➤ **Step 1: Determine if necessary milestones and results are being achieved.**

To determine if your game plan is succeeding or not, it's important to measure your progress on a regular basis. To do so:

❑ Review your game plan pyramid. Ask yourself: Are you and your team achieving the necessary milestones and results with respect to:

___ Achieving team objectives,

___ Implementing work unit methods and systems,

___ Executing individual assignments and tasks,

❑ If not, determine why. Ask:

___ What problems need to be addressed?

___ What lessons have we learned?

___ Are these the right objectives, methods and systems, or individual assignments and tasks?

___ Is something wrong with our approach?

___ Does the team's skill-building plan need to be adjusted?

___ Are there motivational or environmental barriers to team, work unit, and/or individual performance?

➤ **Step 2: Build on your success!**

For each area of success, be sure to ask:

❑ What roles were executed well by team members?

❑ Which methods or systems delivered the desired results?

❑ How did the team's playing style contribute to our success?

❑ What modifications were made to successfully adjust to unforeseen problems?

❑ What are the keys to our success?

❑ What actions do we want to repeat?

Bibliography

Chadwick, David. *The 12 Leadership Principles of Dean Smith*. Kingston: Total/Sports Illustrated, 1999.

Doyel, Gregg. *Coach K: Building the Duke Dynasty: The Story of Mike Krzyzewski and the Winning Tradition at Duke University*. Lenexa, KS: ADDAX Publishing Group, 1999.

Hamm, Mia, and Heifetz, Aaron. *Go For the Goal: A Champion's Guide to Winning in Soccer and Life*. New York: HarperCollins, 1999.

Holtz, Lou. *Winning Every Day: The Game Plan for Success*. New York: HarperBusiness, 1999.

Hunter, Douglas. *Scotty Bowman: A Life in Hockey*. Toronto: Penguin Canada, 1998.

Jones, Charlie. *What Makes Winners Win: Thoughts and Reflections from Successful Athletes*. Secaucus, NJ: Birch Lane Press, 1997.

Maraniss, David. *When Pride Still Mattered: A Life of Vince Lombardi*. New York: Simon & Schuster, 1999.

Miers, Charles, and Trecker, Jim. *Women's Soccer: The Game and the World Cup*. New York: Universe Publishing, 1999.

Riley, Pat. *The Winner Within: A Life Plan for Team Players*. New York: Berkley Publishing Group, 1993.

Walsh, Bill. *Bill Walsh: Finding the Winning Edge.* Champaign, IL: Sports Publishing Inc., 1997.

Wooden, John. *Wooden: A Lifetime of Observations and Reflections On and Off the Court.* Lincolnwood, IL: NTC/Contemporary Publishing, 1997.

Index

DETROIT ROCKIES Kneeling, from left: Michael Robinson, Douglas Jackson, Corey Gaston, Nathan Roberts, Charles Puckett, Corey Brock. Standing, from left: Gloria Meyers (Manager), Alex Gaston (Assistant Coach), Robert Evangelista (Head Coach), Brandon Johnson, Edward Rembert, Louis Ali, Damon Robinson, Greg Adams, Vernon Washington, Brandon Wilkins, Damian Meyers, George Adams, David Slater. Absent: Garreth Warren

From The Detroit News
Detroit Rockies reach respect with Midget hockey title

Corey Gaston, 17, of Detroit, led the Detroit Rockies, a Midget AA hockey team comprised of 15 African-American players, to victory in the Can/Am Challenge Cup in Lake Placid, N.Y. The Rockies beat Cape Cod, Mass., 7-1, in the title game.

The Rockies "are the only all-black hockey team to compete at this level of competition ever in the history of the sport," Rockies Coach Robert Evangelista said.

The Rockies outscored their Lake Placid opponents, 35-8. But winning is not their only goal. "We pursue our one goal: developing good young men," Evangelista said. "We are primarily concerned with the survival of our kids. Discipline, self-control, sound judgment, good manners and respect are taught along with forechecking strategies, faceoff techniques and crisp passing. Winning has been a pleasant byproduct of our work."

From Adirondock Daily Enterprise
Made up of inner city kids, Rockies not the usual hockey team

LAKE PLACID—The Detroit Rockies went undefeated at the Can/Am Hockey Tournament, taking home the gold in the Midget AuSable Division. Although this is a great accomplishment, there is more to this team than just great hockey players.

The team is made up primarily of inner city kids whose team is sponsored by the Police Athletic League (PAL). PAL was designed to help get kids off the streets, and into an environment where they learn a lot more than how to play hockey.

Whether or not they wanted to develop stars, they did. The Rockies have remained together since they were mites. A few players have changed the face of the team slightly, but most of them have been playing as a team for six years.

NEED HELP IMPLEMENTING *THE BUSINESS OF WINNING* IN YOUR ORGANIZATION?

You have the ideas; now turn them into action. Create your own winning game plan in a fun, fast-paced, one-day **management seminar** based on the book. Learn to apply Robert Evangelista's practical process and leave with an action plan and tools to implement a successful business game plan in your organization. For more information, contact The Center for Effective Performance, Inc. at www.cepworldwide.com or call 1-800-558-4CEP.

MORE GREAT BOOKS FROM CEP PRESS

CEP Press is a full-service publisher of performance improvement, training, and management books and tools. All of our publications boast the same high quality and value, and the same practical resources and relevant information that you have come to expect from us.

	Quantity	Price	Total
The Business of Winning A Manager's Guide to Building a Championship Team at Work by Robert Evangelista ($18.95 US, $28.95 CAN)			
Conquering Organizational Change *Available in June 2001* How to Succeed Where Most Companies Fail by Pierre Mourier & Martin Smith ($18.95 US, $28.95 CAN)			
What Every Manager Should Know About Training An Insider's Guide to Getting Your Money's Worth from Training Second edition by Robert F. Mager ($19.95 US, $29.95 CAN)			
Subtotal			
Shipping & Handling			
Canada, GA & TX residents add sales tax to the subtotal plus S&H			
TOTAL ORDER			

U.S. Shipping & Handling: Please add $6 for the first book plus $1.50 for each additional book. Please allow four weeks for ground delivery.

Name _____

Phone _____ **Fax** _____

Organization _____

Address _____

City _____ **State** _____ **ZIP** _____

❑ My check or money order for $_____ is enclosed.

Charge my ❑ Visa ❑ Mastercard ❑ AmEx   Exp. Date _____

Card Number _____

Name on Card _____

Please send this form and your check, money order, or credit card number to:
CEP, P.O. Box 102462, Atlanta, GA 30368-2462

Call 1-800-558-4CEP for volume discount information.

Call for shipping charges on international orders.

For credit card orders, fax this order for faster delivery to (770) 458-9109 or use our Web site: www.ceppress.com